THE
BEST
AMERICAN
POETRY
2001

◇ ◇ ◇

Robert Hass, Editor

David Lehman, Series Editor

SCRIBNER POETRY

NEW YORK   LONDON   TORONTO   SYDNEY   SINGAPORE

SCRIBNER POETRY
1230 Avenue of the Americas
New York, NY 10020

SCRIBNER POETRY and design are trademarks
of Macmillan Library Reference USA, Inc., used under license
by Simon & Schuster, the publisher of this work.

For information regarding special discounts for bulk purchases,
please contact Simon & Schuster Special Sales at 1-800-456-6798 or
business@simonandschuster.com

Manufactured in the United States of America

1   3   5   7   9   10   8   6   4   2

ISBN 0-7432-0383-6
0-7432-0384-4 (Pbk)
ISSN 1040-5763

CONTENTS

David Lehman was born in New York City in 1948. He is the author of five poetry books, including *The Daily Mirror: A Journal in Poetry* (2000) and *The Evening Sun* (forthcoming in 2002), both from Scribner. Among his nonfiction books are *The Last Avant-Garde: The Making of the New York School of Poets* (Anchor, 1999) and *The Perfect Murder* (Michigan, 2000). With Star Black he is coeditor of *The KGB Bar Book of Poems* (HarperCollins, 2000). He has received a Guggenheim Fellowship in poetry, an Academy Award in Literature from the American Academy of Arts and Letters, and a three-year writer's award from the Lila Wallace–Reader's Digest Fund. He is on the core faculty of the graduate writing programs at Bennington College and the New School for Social Research, and teaches "Great Poems" in the undergraduate honors program at NYU. He directs the University of Michigan Press's Poets on Poetry Series. He initiated *The Best American Poetry* in 1988.

FOREWORD

by David Lehman

◊ ◊ ◊

A curious thing has happened. While American poetry continues to
flourish, this has occurred in an inverse relationship to the prestige of
high culture as traditionally understood and measured. High culture has
taken a beating. At regular intervals journalists announce the demise of
the "public intellectual." Stories circulate about dysfunctional English
departments (Duke, Columbia). Outrageous hoaxes bamboozle the
faculty's talking heads, whose peculiar patois and preference for theory
over practice provoke savage indignation in some corners and satirical
merriment in others. A respected professor at a major university told me
that the only thing unifying the warring factions in the English depart-
ment there is "a common hatred of literature." In the twenty-fifth
anniversary issue of *Parnassus: Poetry in Review,* the journal's editor, Her-
bert Leibowitz, laments the dwindling of "the audience for belletristic
criticism—as opposed to the jargon-riddled academic variety." Lei-
bowitz regards poetry criticism as an art, an art in crisis because of bad
academic habits on the one side and the timidity of poets on the other
("the reluctance of poets to write honestly about their peers"). He
surely has a point and is in an excellent position to know. Yet what is
equally noteworthy is that the virus afflicting poetry criticism has left
poetry itself uncontaminated.

In the last decade the audience for poetry has grown; enthusiasts keep
turning up in unexpected quarters, and the media are paying attention
and magnifying the effect. Poetry readings, fairs, and festivals have pro-
liferated. National Poetry Month has raised April sales (without lower-
ing those of other months). Initiatives ranging from "Poetry in Motion"
posters in buses and subways to Robert Pinsky's "favorite poem project"
have helped bridge the gap between poetry and the ordinary citizen. The
radio voice of Garrison Keillor reads a Shakespeare sonnet in drive
time, and on the *News Hour* with Jim Lehrer that evening a retired Air

Force officer tearfully recites Yusef Komunyakaa's poem about the Vietnam Memorial, "Facing It." Are these things causes or effects of the poetry boom? Probably both, as are Bill Moyers's PBS documentaries, *The Language of Life* in 1995 and *Fooling with Words* four years later. Moyers's efforts have met with highbrow derision, but that is true of many efforts to popularize a cultural phenomenon with a reputation for difficulty. One critic has called Moyers the "Bob Costas of the American poetry world," the "ultimate fan," which may be one of those left-handed insults that conveys something of a compliment despite its contemptuous intent. Quarrel with Moyers's taste and judgment all you want; there is no denying the value of his TV programs in building an audience for the poets lucky enough to get air time.

More popular than ever, creative writing programs have helped make up for the neglect of literature elsewhere on campus. It is an argument for the health and vitality of contemporary poetry that so many talented young people devote two graduate years to its study despite knowing that "there's nothing in it" (as Ezra Pound's Mr. Nixon warns in "Hugh Selwyn Mauberley"). It is, of course, easy to mock the locutions of the universal workshop, though I find not only humor but a sort of charm in them. One day in a workshop last February, somebody said, "I had issues with the pronouns in the other lines, too," and off went that little mental explosion that tells me a poem, in the case at hand a villanelle, was on the way. I called it "Issues":

I had issues with the pronouns in the other lines, too.
It started to kick in for me with the part about the war.
Did what I say make sense to you?

I wondered whether what "you" said was true,
Which may have been what "you" were aiming for.
I had issues with the pronouns in the other lines, too,

And not just the pronouns but the branding ("Mountain Dew").
I like the imagery especially "in the forest there's a door."
Did what I say make sense to you?

But I wish the poem didn't dodge the repercussions of "Jew,"
And I winced at "hoodlums and whores."
I had issues with the pronouns in the other lines, too,

But in the other lines what comes through is you,
What I hear is your voice, a kind of quiet roar.
Did what I say make sense to you?

Don't get me wrong, I like the second-person point of view,
But it raises issues. Like what. Like gender.
I had issues with the pronouns in the other lines, too.
Did what I say make sense to you?

As one who teaches workshops I recognize their structural defects. I sometimes wonder how certain great poems would fare in a workshop. I can well imagine that after the class got through with Wallace Stevens's "Of Mere Being" the amazing last line of that poem ("The bird's fire-fangled feathers dangle down") would not survive intact. Nevertheless I'm convinced that the study of poetry, fiction, and serious literature depends more and more on creative writing programs on all levels. This may seem a supreme irony to anyone who remembers the combination of condescension and skepticism that English department regulars directed at their creative writing colleagues twenty-five years ago. Creative writing is sometimes denigrated on the grounds that few workshop-trained poets will go on to write poems as great as those of Wallace Stevens, who studied law, not poetry or creative writing. But few poets, workshop-trained or not, will write great poems. Our mission is to nurture talent and keep the love of poetry at its liveliest, most receptive, and most creative state, and if the student publishes few poems but becomes an avid reader we will have done a job that others have relinquished.

A good deal of creativity has gone into the teaching of creative writing. Low residency MFA programs, such as the ones at Bennington in Vermont and Warren Wilson in North Carolina, which convene for short periods twice a year and do the rest of their work by correspondence between student and faculty, enable grown-ups with families, spouses, jobs to give sustained attention to their writing. Given demographic trends, it is easy to predict the growth of such programs as well as the spread of summer writing conferences lasting anywhere from a weekend to several weeks in picturesque locales. Already the ambitious initiate of whatever age can take instruction at Bread Loaf, Sewanee, Squaw Valley, Saratoga Springs, Provincetown, the Napa Valley, and numerous other desirable sites including the European cities of Prague, St. Petersburg,

Dublin, and Paris. I can hear the retort of the scandalized idealist who associates the creative writing workshop with the decline of civilization: "In the baby boom generation, no one will retire. Instead they will write poetry." Well, maybe, and all of us must sometimes secretly fear that everyone wants to write the stuff and no one wants to read it. At such moments we would do well to recall that Seamus Heaney's verse translation of *Beowulf*, not your conventional potboiler, sold two hundred thousand copies in hardcover and occupied a slot on the *New York Times* bestseller list for ten weeks last year. Readers do exist, more than you might have thought. The trick remains how to reach them.

On the "everyone wants to write the stuff" front, New York Mets' reliever Turk Wendell, he of the animal-claw necklace, writes it ("Life Is Like a Baseball"). Monica Lewinsky moved to New York and came out in favor of "The Love Song of J. Alfred Prufrock," which she imitated (loosely) in a Valentine's Day poem commissioned by a British magazine. Paul McCartney is writing a book of poems. Julia Roberts has written poems for years and particularly loves Neruda. Ashley Judd, who memorizes a poem for each birthday, chose Wordsworth's "Daffodils" last year and is leaning this year toward Rudyard Kipling's "If." Kim Cattrall, who plays Samantha in the HBO hit *Sex and the City,* likes reciting Rupert Brooke while her boyfriend plays the string bass. Helen Hunt says she is "obsessed with Rilke." Her favorite "is an untitled one in a collection that Robert Bly translated," which she proceeds to paraphrase: "I want to unfold because where I am closed I am false; I want to be with those who know secret things or else alone." David Duchovny, who studied with Harold Bloom at Yale, has never made a secret of his admiration of John Ashbery's "Self-Portrait in a Convex Mirror." Asked by a *Movieline* reporter to analyze the poem, the star of *The X-Files* gladly obliged: "It's about a man who's painting his self-portrait, but he's looking into a mirrored ball, and the closer he gets to it, the further away his image seems to be going." Duchovny then drew a parallel between the poem's posture and his own style as an actor: "I'm trying to protect what I advertise. That's my stance on any kind of self-expression."

I have a cultivated interest in the unusual ways people use poetry in their public or professional lives. Last year did not disappoint. Dona Nieto, a California performance artist who calls herself La Tigresa, bared her breasts and declaimed "goddess-based, nude Buddhist guerilla poetry" at timber sites north of San Francisco to protest the logging of ancient redwoods. Anonymous cyber-scribes adapted familiar lines by

Longfellow, Poe, Whitman, Ogden Nash, Joyce Kilmer, Alfred Noyes, and Clement Moore to satirize the post-election stalemate in Florida. Salman Rushdie in the *Guardian* versified the electoral results in the manner of Dr. Seuss. (Aided by "the great Legal Grinches, / and Grinches of Spin," the Grinch exhorts his cohorts to "Grinch / This election!") On TV, a contestant on *Who Wants to Be a Millionaire?* won $2,000 for shrewdly relying on the audience to know that the number of lines in a couplet is two. In one episode of the TV drama *Bull,* a ruthless tycoon quotes Yeats ("But one man loved the pilgrim soul in you, / And loved the sorrows of your changing face"), while in a different scene a bearded financial shark tosses off an allusion to Edna St. Vincent Millay ("My candle burns at both ends") to ridicule a Smith College alumna during a game of "humiliate the host." In HBO's hit series *The Sopranos,* Anthony, Jr., listens as his older sister, Meadow, a Columbia freshman, knowingly explains the symbolism of the snow in Frost's "Stopping by Woods on a Snowy Evening." "That's fucked up," her brother replies. If you get a chance to see Melissa Palmer's movie *Wildflowers,* you'll note that the guest editor of this year's *Best American Poetry* plays a poet named Robert who gets to recite his poems and court the character played by Daryl Hannah.

After the Los Angeles Lakers won the NBA championship in June 2000, Shaquille O'Neal quoted Shakespeare's "Some are born great, some achieve greatness, and some have greatness thrust upon them" at a victory celebration. While the Lakers' center left it unstated how these lines applied to the situation at hand, none could deny their grandeur. A few months earlier coach Phil Jackson had made a gift to O'Neal of Nietzsche's selected writings. "He was ahead of his time," O'Neal said. "Everybody else was analog and Nietzsche was digital." As the stock market swooned, Charles Millard, the former head of Internet investment banking at Prudential Securities, turned to Keats to explain the inevitable discrepancy between actual and anticipated profits. "Heard melodies are sweet, but those unheard / Are sweeter," Millard quoted, adding: "That reality is now hitting people right in the face." When a jail sentence smacked Dana C. Giacchetto, formerly Leonardo di Caprio's financial advisor, he took up poetry. Sample line: "At the nexus where art meets justice, a chemistry dancing like angels sweating with peace, yet, halfway asleep." Now there's a man who could benefit from a poetry writing workshop.

The Best American Poetry is committed to the notion that excellence in poetry is not incompatible with the pursuit of a general audience. Robert Hass, who succeeded Rita Dove as U. S. poet laureate and now succeeds her as the guest editor of this anthology, has dedicated himself to this project with the zeal that has characterized his efforts over the years to promote literature and literacy on the widest level. As poet laureate Hass, a distinguished critic as well as poet, wrote a weekly column ("The Poet's Choice") for the *Washington Post* recommending poets and poems in language direct and unaffected, adjectives not usually associated with critical writing; he would print the poem in full and comment briefly on it, careful not to let the commentary eclipse the verse. (When, after 212 weeks without a break, Hass gave up the column in January 2000, it was, fittingly, Dove who took it over.) Back when I asked him if he would undertake the editing of this anthology, Hass described himself as the "Raskolnikov of deadlines." After working with him on *The Best American Poetry 2001,* I am able to attest to the justness of this epithet—and to say that working with him was worth stretching any number of deadlines.

In the year 2000, as the IPO market crashed and one dot-com after another went under, some of us cherished all the more such "old economy" staples as books and magazines. Yet for poetry, which resists being turned into a commodity, the Internet remains a particularly friendly and potentially transformative space, offering a revolutionary means and method of publication and distribution. You can't help but admire the energy and enterprise informing electronic magazines and literary Web sites such as *Slate, Salon, The Cortland Review, Poetry Daily, Nerve, Pif, Can We Have Our Ball Back?* (its title evidently a nod to the Beatles' movie *A Hard Day's Night*), and most improbably two different 'zines named after Arthur Rimbaud's poem, "Le Bateau ivre" ("The Drunken Boat"). Both are brand-new. The one edited by Ravi Shankar (not the sitar player but a recent graduate of Columbia's MFA program) is called *Drunken Boat* (at www.drunkenboat.com) in contrast to the one edited by Rebecca Seiferle, a contributor to *The Best American Poetry 2000,* which is *The Drunken Boat* (at www.thedrunkenboat.com). It was in general an excellent year for Rimbaud, whose "Une Saison en enfer" ("A Season in Hell") is quoted by Marcia Gay Harden playing Lee Krasner in Ed Harris's movie *Pollock.*

This is the fifteenth volume in *The Best American Poetry* series. I have had many occasions to celebrate the accomplishments or recognitions of the fifteen guest editors to date. But until this year I have not had to mourn the passing of one of them. A. R. Ammons died on February 25,

2001, a week after his seventy-fifth birthday. "We're gliding," he wrote in the concluding lines of *Sphere: The Form of a Motion*. "We

are gliding: ask the astronomer, if you don't believe it: but
motion as a summary of time and space is gliding us: for a while,
we may ride such forces: then, we must get off: but now this

beats any amusement park by the shore: our Ferris wheel, what a
wheel: our roller coaster, what mathematics of stoop and climb: sew
my name on my cap: we're clear: we're ourselves: we're sailing."

Robert Hass was born in San Francisco in 1941. He grew up in Marin County and attended St. Mary's College of California and Stanford University. *Field Guide,* his first book, was selected by Stanley Kunitz as the winner of the Yale Younger Poets competition for 1973. Three subsequent collections have appeared: *Praise* (1979), *Human Wishes* (1989), and *Sun Under Wood* (1996), all from the Ecco Press. *Sun Under Wood* won the National Book Critics Circle prize in poetry. A book of essays, *Twentieth-Century Pleasures: Prose on Poetry* (1984), had previously won the National Book Critics Circle prize in criticism. Hass, the recipient of a MacArthur Fellowship, has long collaborated with Czeslaw Milosz on the translations of his poems. He has also edited a volume of Tomas Tranströmer's selected poems and he edited and translated most of the contents of *The Essential Haiku: Versions of Basho, Buson, and Issa.* For two years starting in 1995, he served as the nation's poet laureate. Both during and after his appointment, he has worked tirelessly to promote literacy and to protect the environment. For many years he taught at St. Mary's College and is now a professor at the University of California, Berkeley.

INTRODUCTION

by Robert Hass

◇　◇　◇

It was August when I finally got down to the business of this anthology. I had been reading literary magazines for months; David Lehman, the editor of the *Best American Poetry* series, had also been reading, and sending me quite regularly, like news bulletins, his cullings from dozens of literary magazines, some of them hallowed and of long standing, some of them new and completely, even intentionally, obscure. I had imagined, when I was asked to edit this book, and I do mean *imagined,* a year that resolved itself into a procession of quiet and orderly evenings in which I finished dinner, did the dishes, took a short walk in the weathers as they changed, and then sat down in a comfortable chair, in a circle of lamplight, and read a year's worth of the poems of my time with immense clarity of mind.

It was my usual mistake. I had not so much agreed to undertake a task as I had signed up to be the main character in a poem by Wallace Stevens with a title like "The Room Was Quiet and the World Was Calm." The room was not quiet and the world is not calm, and I was in the poem by Emily Dickinson that I'd been in in the first place, the one that begins: "A Day! Help! Help! Another Day!" And I don't think I was even the main character. There are hundreds of literary magazines in America, as well as many general interest magazines that publish poetry. Many of them are quarterlies, so had I had my succession of nights like days in the peaceable kingdom, I would have had the task of reading at least one new magazine a night for three hundred and sixty-five days. Some of those magazines—like the special summer poetry issue of the *Paris Review*—contained as many as a hundred poems, whereas an environmental journal like *Wild Earth* or a political weekly like *The Nation* printed only two or three. One way and another, it is a lot of poetry. I went at it mostly in fitful attacks, binges, when I found I had a few hours, whatever the time of day. Mostly I just marked poems that I liked well enough to return to. Some days, it seemed, I liked everything I read. Some days I liked nothing. I had no clear sense how much of this was mood and how much the quality of the work I happened to be reading. It was not the ideal circumstance in which to read poetry, but the magazines were full of interest and, though I felt some anxiety about the final shape of the project, I liked doing the reading.

That there was so much poetry to be read I took to be a sign of cultural health. It meant a lot of people were literate and alive. You have to have some kind of interior life to make a work of art and in a world as busy and heedless as this one we need all the consciousness we can muster. Think of it this way. On my bookshelf there's an anthology of seventeenth-century American poetry. It's almost entirely the poetry of the New England colonies and it's over five hundred pages long. At least two poets from that time—Anne Bradstreet and Edward Taylor— wrote real poems, poems that can be read today for more than scholarly or antiquarian reasons. There are fifty-one poets in all published in the book and a substantial selection of anonymous poems. There were about a hundred thousand people in New England in 1700. So—if this were in any sense a sample human population: think of all the ways in which it wasn't; they had a world to build from scratch—this would imply that you might get two poets of unusual gifts and fifty or so poets in all in a population that size. If that were true, then there ought to be in the United States three hundred years later, with its three hundred million population, at least six thousand poets with some special talent and one hundred fifty thousand people or so who occasionally write poems. Of course, the gene pool doesn't seem to work in quite that way. But you take my point. There are more literate people in Kansas City today than there were in Shakespeare's London. There's no reason why every American city should not produce a writer of great interest to the rest of us.

This reflection engendered others. Anne Bradstreet produced the first book of published poetry by a North American. The book was printed in England and it was called *The Tenth Muse*. It consisted mainly of long, learned poems on themes of interest to seventeenth-century Protestants and very few people would have any interest in reading it today. The poems of hers that people do read are a few short personal poems written to her family. They have a fresh, intimate directness and simplicity and Anne Bradstreet seems to have thought them too personal for publication. They found their way into print in the middle of the nineteenth century, two hundred years after her death. Edward Taylor, who was a frontier minister, wrote very learned and bookish, but also homely and sometimes quite wild, devotional poetry. He did this apparently as a spiritual practice. He produced a couple of hundred of these poems, lines written preparatory to his receiving the Lord's Supper, bound them in a leather book of his own making, but did not publish them and asked his children not to publish them. They were discovered in the Yale University Library in the 1930s and published after that.

As everyone knows, Emily Dickinson published a handful of poems in her lifetime. When she died, her sister found a boxful of carefully composed small booklets in her hand made of thick folded paper. They contained over a thousand poems. Four hundred of them or so are among the four hundred best poems ever written in the English language. She died in 1886. Some of the poems were published in 1890. There was not a thorough scholarly collection of her work until 1955, the year before Allen Ginsberg published *Howl* as a paperback book, then a distinctly subrespectable format, issued by a small bookstore in the Italian district of San Francisco. I don't know whether "Howl" ever appeared in a magazine, but it seems unlikely that, had there been a *Best American Poetry* volume of 1956, it would have appeared there. Walt Whitman, Emily Dickinson's contemporary, and the other founding genius of American poetry, published his first book with a small press that specialized in odd Victorian versions of New Age fads: ocean bathing and reading people's characters from the bumps on their heads. It was published in 1855, the year, as everyone likes to notice, of Longfellow's "Hiawatha," which would certainly have made it into the *Best American Poetry* of 1855. As for Dickinson, her poems were not available for publication, but any imaginary and retrospective *Best American Poetry* of 1862 or 1863 would have to consist of seventy poems by Emily Dickinson (Walt Whitman did not write much in those two years) and a little room for others, out of what she liked to call "civility."

All of which is to say that, as the poems were piling up, I had no great confidence that I was going to reflect accurately the best poetry written in the past year. The present is notoriously blind to itself in the first place. And, more pertinent to my ruminations, America has this history of buried and recovered poets. I'm not clear about the reasons, but they must combine at least two facts. One is that poetry is a very private kind of art. One can generalize about the health or direction of "American Poetry" at any given moment, as if it were a corporate enterprise, but it isn't in the end a team sport. The resonances of American poetry, like the resonances of our great song lyrics, "April is the cruelest month," "After great pain a formal feeling comes," "I hate to see that evening sun go down," speak to our collective experience but they do so, almost always, in tones that come, unmistakably, from depth and silence. So that poetry not only can turn up just about anywhere, just about anywhere is where it is most likely to turn up.

The second reason is the fact of American space, the great distances between our metropolitan cultures. In Europe and in Asia, it would seem, written poetry flowered wherever the center of learning was, especially if it was also a center of commercial vitality. And each culture— even one as vast as China—seemed to have one cultural center, which was also the center of political power. Poetry in Sweden is mostly Stockholm, in Korea mostly Seoul. Boston is still the representative city of learning in America and New York the world capital, the center of publishing, of commerce, often of innovation, always of fashionable opinion. In the arts judgment has always tended to issue from critics writing in East Coast journals and from professors at eastern universities, literary reputations got made in the publishing houses and reviewing organs in New York. Chicago had its own vitality, and, in the early years of the century, its own gathering of poets and one of the world's most important literary magazines in the *Poetry* of Harriet Monroe and Ezra Pound. Briefly, in the 1950s and 1960s San Francisco became a kind of alternative staging center for the energies of a new generation of poets. And Los Angeles became the capital of the glamor of commercial entertainment, movies, and music.

The young have been heading to cities to get educated, for learning and for style and for sexiness and for jobs, probably since Theocritus left Sicily for Alexandria two thousand years ago. As soon as there was writing, and jobs to be had as scribes, the young went to cities and started making poetry. And, of course, it still happens in America and a few cities—probably just these few, Boston, New York, Chicago, Los Angeles, San Francisco—draw young artists who gather there and invent themselves into schools. But creative writing programs have changed that pattern in ways that still seem unpredictable. If Sherwood Anderson's *Winesburg, Ohio* is accurate, to be a person with an imagination in a small American town at the turn of the twentieth century meant that you would, eventually, some spring night, end up running down the street in the middle of the night naked and screaming. Now those people, growing up in all the towns and suburbs of the continent, can find their way to a local college, some place that has art studios and a music scene and a poetry or fiction writing class. Poets are likely for this reason to turn up anywhere, or not turn up, not be in the midst of making a splash on some literary scene known to the scanners that devise literary reputation as 'the state of American poetry.'

And here I was, one of those scanners, about to sit down on a bright summer morning, a cup of coffee in hand, and take out the boxes of marked-up magazines and xeroxes of poems from magazines, my own markings and the xeroxes and notations of the indefatigable David Lehman, and try to find what I was looking for. I'd read a lot of poems I liked, many poems very different from each other and of a similar quality. There are roughly three traditions in American poetry at this point: a metrical tradition that can be very nervy and that is also basically classical in impulse; a strong central tradition of free verse made out of both romanticism and modernism, split between the impulses of an inward and psychological writing and an outward and realist one, at its best fusing the two; and an experimental tradition that is usually more passionate about form than content, perception than emotion, restless with the conventions of the art, skeptical about the political underpinnings of current practice, and intent on inventing a new one, or at least undermining what seems repressive in the current formed style. Traditions, of course, are always in flux, and the best work is often being done in the interstices between them. At the moment, there are poets doing good, bad, and indifferent work in all these ranges. I had marked for rereading a couple of hundred poems and I had David's sometimes overlapping lists. I needed either to declare that my taste today was going to be definitive, or I needed a principle of selection. Reading for a while, I was aware that David had, on the whole, favored a poetry of wit and that I, on the whole, had singled out poems that were a little spiky or raw, and intellectually demanding. He was drawn to charm and I had been drawn away from it. I needed an idea. I was looking for what Ezra Pound called, as he was trying to find his way in the *Cantos,* "the rose in the steel dust."

What gave me a way in was coming across in succession some posthumously published poems by Elizabeth Bishop and one by James Schuyler. There was also one by Joseph Brodsky, written in Russian when he was in prison in the 1960s but translated into English in the last American years of his life and found among his papers. I did not in the end reprint the Brodsky poem—I ruled out translations at a certain point in the process, regretfully. Brodsky was a presence in American poetry and there are other poets like Czeslaw Milosz toweringly, and the younger Polish poet Adam Zagajewski and the Slovene Tomaž Šalamun who teach sometimes at American universities and whose work is regularly translated and published here. I would have liked to include their work; it would have said something about the life of poetry in America. I would also have liked to include some English and Irish poets—particularly Irish poets like Paul Muldoon and Seamus Heaney and Eavan Boland who teach regularly in this country. In the end, crowded for room, I was looking for reasons to exclude poets and ruled out the European poets, both the ones who wrote in English and the ones who didn't, and a couple of Latin American poets I might have included, like the Mexican Alberto Blanco, and also the Chinese poet Bei Dao. I had a glimpse, looking in that direction of what might have been done by including work in translation by American poets, especially translation of their contemporaries, so that this anthology would have had running through it like a rift of ore, Forrest Gander's translations of the Mexican poet Pura Lopez Colome, or Lyn Hejinian's translations of Russian experimental poets or Norma Coles's translations of new French poetry or John Balaban's translations from Vietnamese. The mix of poets drawn here from elsewhere—by exile, by cultural curiosity, by the salaries at American universities—and the foreign poets being studied and translated by American poets would have been one kind of portrait of the culture—I had to let it go.

But for the morning I entertained the idea of beginning the book with poems by Bishop, Schuyler, and Brodsky. There seemed something very pure about it. You want new poems. Here are new poems, new in the way that things read for the first time are new, and also in that other way, of the freshness of poetry. There was also some notion in it of the dead no longer having the fevered literary world at stake. They were in the place, it seemed, that Auden had spoken of when he said that poetry survived in the valley of its saying. Reading literary magazines for poems, one also reads the essays and reviews. Poetry may not be a team sport, but you would not know it from the magazines. Young poets school up, for support. They are also inclined to be competitive, and moralistic about it, convinced that any writing that is not doing exactly what they're doing is morally reprehensible. The shrillest, it often seems—Ezra Pound is the great counterexample—are the mediocre writers to whom only the allegiance of a school and a method gives legitimacy. It's one of the reasons why Milosz, in a moment of either impatience or conviction, called literature a tournament of hunchbacks. Many of the magazines this season had something of that tone; the polemics in literary cyberspace had even more. Poets sniping at each other not only about the purity of their literary technique but about the sources of their income. In one particularly mullahlike exchange, an eminent critic complained that a well-known poet of antirealist tendency had sold out by appearing on the same stage with an elder European poet who had a realistic aesthetic. The presence of Bishop and Schuyler, both very private poets, less than expansive, in their different ways domestic and meticulous, both writers whom, I always felt, wrote as if they had psychic wounds they needed to work around rather than confront—a tactic I did not judge; who is to tell someone else how to survive in such intimate territory?—seemed to me to give my imaginary anthology a tone I could begin to hear. It spoke to something essentially private in poetry communicated one-on-one from writer to reader, and also something about the way ego is burned off by writing absorbed in its task, and of course it touched with what felt to me a certain coolness a central mystery of art, that it is human utterance, or gesture, that sometimes survives death. I had no way of knowing if these poems would outlive their generation, but here in this book they stand for that possibility—poems about what? eros, the oddness of a sense of place.

The next thing that caught my eye, connected probably to these considerations, was that among the poems I had clipped there were a large number of poems by the poets I had grown up, or had grown into poetry, reading, that were about, in different ways, the changes of age. It's a strangeness, I suppose, that belongs to any generation that one ages watching the artists a half a generation older than oneself go from being the young ones to being the old ones. It is not easy to age in America, as many people have observed. But it is, it seems, easy enough to age in poetry. It's not downhill skiing, or mathematics for that matter which seems to use up its talents quite young. As longevity has increased, there has grown up in American poetry a considerable body of work made by older artists—the late poems of Wallace Stevens and Hilda Doolittle and William Carlos Williams and Robinson Jeffers, even the final fragmentary *Cantos* of Ezra Pound come to mind—that has solidity and strength, sometimes brilliance or wisdom. One is grateful for it in the fathers and mothers. But it is odd to see it in the older brothers and sisters, especially that rowdy generation that came of age in the 1950s and 1960s. Many of them are gone, of course. Allen Ginsberg and Frank O'Hara and Sylvia Plath and James Wright and Charles Olson and Denise Levertov and James Merrill. And just this year Gregory Corso and Gwendolyn Brooks and A. R. Ammons. There was in them a mix of impulses—they were radicals and mandarins and swells, wild ones, populists, aesthetes and isolatos, masters of the perfected or the apparently tossed-off gesture.

As a generation, they were my way into contemporary poetry—from the middle of high school, really, when the newspapers in San Francisco were full of stories about the Beat generation and the trial to keep a lewd book called *Howl* out of the innocent American mind, they were the poets I read to understand the rhythms of time in the time I was growing into. Harold Bloom remarked in an introduction to one of these anthologies that the ideal reader of poetry was a superbly educated one. Maybe so. But a person has to get there somehow, and there is something to be said for the youthful and ignorant reader. It seems to me that at a certain point in my early reading of poetry I had a kind of attention in which, as in sex, the minute became huge. Every oddness of line ending, stutter of rhythm, intricacy of music, or—think of early John Ashbery—resolute flatness of tone seemed momentous. There is, I suppose, a certain narcissism in this. One is waking to oneself and to the poetry at once. It's a time when you also begin to learn the range of ideas that can instigate a poetry. There was a time, I remember, when I first went to poetry readings and was often offended that the poets reading their own poems did not sound like they were supposed to sound, that is, did not sound as they sounded in my head. I formed the idea then that the poems were superior to the poets and that I, as their disinterested reader, was more faithful to the poems than the poets were, who had gone on to the next poem or the next stage of their lives. So it was affecting, as I went through the magazines again, to see how many poems there were about aging, or about time and change, by the writers of that generation—from Kenneth Koch's delicious and complicated ode to the Second World War to Grace Paley's wry notational lyric to the poems of Richard Howard and John Hollander and Anthony Hecht, three of the generation's formalists, to Galway Kinnell's palpably physical meditation on decomposition as a central part of the world's work.

These poems became for me the idea of a stratum or layer in this book. I thought at first of beginning with the dead poets and ending with the living older poets, and then organizing the anthology in rough chronological order by decades, so that the very young would come at the beginning. It is an interesting time for young poets. They've inherited an aesthetic or set of aesthetics in which the basic relationship to language has become the central problem and it has given their work, so far, its particular forms of playfulness and tortuousness, interest and opacity and risk. Partly they're reacting against what has come to seem effortless and therefore indulgent in a previous generation, the poem of incident in plain language, which aims at a certain sincerity of address and tone, as if life was exactly the size of the self and consisted of a set of serial epiphanies. Some of this echoes the influence of the critical tradition in European philosophy in the universities, some of it is the ground-clearing required of any oppositional art. In this case, because it's suspicious of subject matter as such, suspicious, as I've seen it described, of the "aboutness" of poetry, it's preoccupied with issues of style, with the relationship therefore between language and perception. It also goes largely on instinct and the instinct is that some right, cool, strange, or estranged ferocity of language would catch the instability of things and undo, in its utopian versions, if not the whole global economy at least the self-satisfied clichés which present that vision of power in the world as triumphant and inevitable. Any young art—think of Rembrandt's early self-portrait—has an element in it of showboating, of display, fury and display, or mockery and display, hilarity and display, or woundedness and irony and display, but it often has, ought maybe to have, the exuberance of young artists coming to the medium, and I thought that would sit interestingly against the poems of Bishop and Schuyler who were beyond that impulse, or had turned it into something else. So an idea of an anthology was coming into focus. In the end I don't think I've represented the younger poets nearly as well as I would have liked. To some extent they got crowded out when I began to read the poets of my own generation. But I hope there is enough of this work so that readers will feel the restlessness and force of what's coming.

Another truth of this kind of reading is that it was a great pleasure to revisit the poets whose work I knew well, the ones who were beginning to publish as I began to publish. I was aware that this more than anything made it difficult for me to come to anything like the objectivity—the transparent-eyeball clarity of mind—I had imagined I could bring to this process. If I mentally conjured a *Best American Poetry 1924* or *1949,* there would be, I was sure, very good poems by poets who were not the poets I had read and read, poems that were in some ways better than the poems written in those years by the artists I have most studied and lived with, but the truth is, I think, that a lesser poem by Wallace Stevens or Marianne Moore would seize my attention because I was interested in and had some feeling for the whole enterprise of their art. They may not have written their most achieved poems in some given year, but they were poets who did not fail to interest me. I knew this was the case with reading my contemporaries. I was aware that, with some poets whose work I knew only casually, I would like a poem well enough to set it aside to reread, but I lacked a sense of its context in their work. There is a way in which the poems in a literary magazine—or an anthology—can be like pieces of luggage on an airport carrel. They go by: an awful lot of them very much alike, various of them distinctive in their way, but in no relation to the others or, in an odd way, to themselves. They have specificity without character whereas a piece of luggage you recognize, your own, or a lover's, or a friend's, or a child's, seems inimitably battered or elegant or mutedly stylish or functional or eccentric. Others are going to have to make of my choices what they make of them—many readers will be reading them with a fresher eye than mine, but I found that there were a large number of poems that gave me pleasure, seemed to have inventive force, or intellectual passion or surprise. I was amused by the sudden raucous rhyming, for example, in Lyn Hejinian. I had a sense of the trajectory that brought Yusef Komunyakaa to the compact odelike song form he brought to the subject of the seven deadly sins. I'm interested in every stage of Louise Glück's art so that a quality austere and hieratic, but also summary and dryly wistful I thought I sensed in her recent work moved me. It interested me that Michael Palmer's poem—his poems are always beautifully written, they often have a quality of comic or mesmerized philosophical opacity—seemed for him unusually direct and that John Koethe's seemed so intentionally to invoke the later manner of Wallace Stevens. This part of the choosing seemed like gathering a party of friends. Some of them in fact are my friends. Others are people whom I hardly know at all and whose work I know in considerable detail. Several of the poets I admire most aren't here, for one reason or another, but the range of work in my generation is represented, I think. I would have liked to have a clear sense of common themes or common preoccupations in this layer of the work, but if they're here I don't have a feeling for them. I thought of it as the work of experienced poets who had been at it long enough to have acquired a fate and who were engaged in the process of making sense of that fate toward the end of the middle of their lives.

This was the point at which I stopped imagining that I would try to talk David Lehman and the editors at Scribner into abandoning the format of this series, which requires that the poems appear in alphabetical order by author. I thought that the generations were going to be a rhythm of this book, also some attempt given my own tastes to represent the range of styles and preoccupations within the generations. In addition to this, I had made a point of picking a certain number of poems by people whose names I didn't recognize. I think there were at least a dozen of these. I wanted long poems and short lyrics. David and I negotiated the impulse to include poems that were accessible and immediately appealing with poems that expected a good deal of readers and gave them therefore the chance to get lost, to get lost and found. It seemed the best thing once there was a map in my head to scramble it. They say that the aesthetic pleasure of cities has to do with the helter-skelter quality of their development on the one hand and the fixity of the grid pattern of streets on the other and the way that mixture of randomness and order keeps tossing up visual surprises. It began to seem to me that this would be the best principle here.

I had months more of reading to do and so did David Lehman. (I read his poems and was informed that he had ruled himself out of appearing in the series he's been shepherding.) I also began not to trust my eye and asked several young poets to reread the whole year's worth of poems and make their selection of poems—I wanted to see with some other sets of eyes. These poets were Jessica Fisher and Brian Glazer and Jennifer Scappettone and Tim Woods, and I want to thank them here. When David asked me to do this work, I think I pointed out that there were whole centuries in which there weren't seventy-five good poems. By the end I was trying to talk him into a format that included eighty-five poems, or eighty, or, my last pitch, seventy-eight, just three more, why not? what's the difference? It didn't happen. A form is a form, and what you have here is seventy-five poems which I hope will convey a sense that there are a dozen or so more poems that are clamoring at the silent wall to be let in.

It would be good if that force were felt by readers coming to this volume as an instance of the force with which human beings seem to need to represent themselves, to make symbols out of their experience, to say what it is like to be themselves, to make things that have not been made before and to bring them into the world and alter the world by doing so, to protest or celebrate the terms of existence, or at least not to go through it mute.

THE
BEST
AMERICAN
POETRY
2001

◇　◇　◇

Notes for a Sermon
on the Mount

◇   ◇   ◇

1. Pussies are not gods. They are created beings.
2. Unlike god, they do not always exist.
3. Dignified, majestic, intelligent, we must attend to them nonetheless.
4. Like all spiritual beings, pussies cannot be seen with the human eye at just any time of day.
5. Pussies represent both the visible and the invisible, the sacred and the profane.
6. They appear to be nowhere and everywhere at once. To be personal and impersonal, human and divine.
7. In the occult story of Adam and Eve, God placed a sword-bearing angel at the entrance of the divine pussy to keep the unwary from ever returning.
8. Revelations describe them as being "robed in a cloud with a rainbow over their heads."
9. Many times a pussy has taken on the form of an actual woman and is sometimes mistakenly thought to have a human spirit.
10. One must not forget to entertain strangers, for by doing so, one might entertain a pussy without even knowing it.
11. Always remember: one must never pray to pussies. Or other golden heifers.
12. Nor should one ask God to send forth a pussy to help minister to one's soul.
13. A pussy must come of its own accord. For thus is the way of the pussy, and of the alpha and omega.

from *Another Chicago Magazine*

The Plan

◇　◇　◇

"Who told you
you were visible?"

God said,

meaning naked
or powerless.

★

We had planned this meeting
in advance,

how we'd address each other,

how we'd stand
or kneel.

Thus our intentions
are different

from our bodies,
something extra,

though transparent
like a negligee.

★

Though a bit sketchy,

like this palm's
impression of a tree—

flashing scales,

on the point of
retraction.

But *sweet.*
You don't understand!

Like a lariat made of scalloped bricks

circling a patch
of grass

from *American Poetry Review*

JOHN ASHBERY

Crossroads in the Past

◇   ◇   ◇

That night the wind stirred in the forsythia bushes,
but it was a wrong one, blowing in the wrong direction.
"That's silly. How can there be a wrong direction?
'It bloweth where it listeth,' as you know, just as we do
when we make love or do something else there are no rules for."

I tell you, something went wrong there a while back.
Just don't ask me what it was. Pretend I've dropped the subject.
No, now you've got me interested, I want to know
exactly what seems wrong to you, how something could

seem wrong to you. In what way do things get to be wrong?
I'm sitting here dialing my cellphone
with one hand, digging at some obscure pebbles with my shovel
with the other. And then something like braids will stand out,

on horsehair cushions. That armchair is really too lugubrious.
We've got to change all the furniture, fumigate the house,
talk our relationship back to its beginnings. Say, you know
that's probably what's wrong—the beginnings concept, I mean.
I aver there are no beginnings, though there were perhaps some
sometime. We'd stopped, to look at the poster the movie theater

had placed freestanding on the sidewalk. The lobby cards
drew us in. It was afternoon, we found ourselves
sitting at the end of a row in the balcony; the theater was unexpectedly
crowded. That was the day we first realized we didn't fully

know our names, yours or mine, and we left quietly
amid the gray snow falling. Twilight had already set in.

from *The New York Review of Books*

Jazz

◇ ◇ ◇

I'd like to know everything
A jazz artist knows, starting with the song
"Goodbye Pork Pie Hat."

Like to make some songs myself:
"Goodbye Rickshaw,"
"Goodbye Lemondrop,"
"Goodbye Rendezvous."

Or maybe even blues:

If you fall in love with me I'll make you pancakes
All morning. If you fall in love with me
I'll make you pancakes all night.
If you don't like pancakes
We'll go to the creperie. If you don't like pancakes
We'll go to the creperie.
If you don't like to eat, handsome boy,
Don't you hang around with me.

On second thought, I'd rather find
The fanciest music I can, and hear all of it.

I'd rather love somebody
And say his name to myself every day
Until I fall apart.

from *The Nebraska Review*

Crossed-Over, Fiend-Snitched, X-ed Out

◇ ◇ ◇

O Sweetie, O Hon, in this weather—split sea pea,
green horizon, mended infinitude—sweet
the lips licking the honeyed, the candy-

coated, the sugared-up. O sweet
those inscrutable untruths. Let me have another
sip of nectar.

Now the wind shifts
the bees downstream; they float, wings dread-drenched.
This is pretty too. This death

set, this cool cup and saucer, clinked
in the mustachioed moment. May I have a little
more? Flutter. Flail.

A stark stake is down driven, a megalith marker
masks the lack. Wreath on the head
of whom? The child is loved

in narcissistic longing to be and to be (again).
That too is translated
onto the stage, the screen. A plane dives. O that?

That's the Twentieth Century, sputtering
its hind parts. The plurality of premises, of needle drop
chandelier tears in a ceiling rose

well over their heads. The planned dance
where one leg crosses
the other. A curtsy. A bow. O anachronym.

We are only here to help you.
We are only here
with our Tarot cards, with our wooden Egyptian

figures, an entire antiquity collection
constructed in a room recess. The outrageous dawning
of opinion—swayable, swayed. Suede

brushes against the train
as it enters the opening, a napkinish ring with a we portrait
of the wedded couple. And then it exits

and we with it. We've been. But where?
Brief picture postcard with a date firm in its intention
to detail. Head bent

over the slate at the rigorosum,
a fertilizing dew collecting at the brink of the lip.
That famous scene from the life of____

comes to mind, the reek of lilac and laburnum.

from *New American Writing*

When the Gods Put on Meter

◇   ◇   ◇

I cleared mother's apartment of her urine-soaked rags today, while she wept.
She wanted to keep them, you see.
She will make more so long as she lives, an hour,

      o loveliest of forms that I may behold you an hour,

      Wife of the Gaze, Husband of the Breath,
      Gleam on the round side of the tear.

★

A woman is dead in the house across the river.
River of shudders river of quivering grief.

  O hummingbirds who drank from her tower of red,
  know that the Queen of Red River is dead.

  Her pink-haired doll, ape, and pony have fled
  through the dresser mirror, as on a pickup bed,

  but stare back the while, as if it's not too late
  to see the Jean moon rise

    —o gods of the ear, is it meter you love?—

        to dazzle Fate,

  the Alien doll who hauls them off, whose eyes ate
  the room and frightened them, such lonely hate!

The widow Jean will never again open
a window in the Castle Ibuprofen

and float out over dress-ups of snow on
the noble firs of Foss River Grove. In

the morning she thought her husband had spoken.
Now every bone in the darkness is broken.

★

What would you regulate—
        the tiny plenitude of "spontaneous" symbols?
The arrhythmical mass writing of the rain?

                oh loveliest of forms

Every bone in the rain is broken

★

You were born in the glade of an averted Eye,
you dressed before the mirror of a hundred arteries—
        oh, don't confuse your arm
with those hanging waters!
        Not *that* leg, the carrot
                        of the downward path!

You learned to desire from where you would never quite be,
        pressed against the flat side of the tear.

★

Where is the rescue?
Cornered children call you River Platte,
your loafshaped covered wagons in their eyes.

Where is the rescue?
Mothers run out to bring in the oxygen
    of the laundry,
shaking themselves into beauty they cannot see.

40

Do you pick it up, broken-headed animal
            and blow on its snow-light fur?

I look into the rain barrel of grief
                        and see that it is raining.

★

How frail is our world:

        by day, caramel forests
        lift their green travels. At night,
        quartets of sparks
        fly down to us,
        the coals of the Offering.
        The moon is given
        and taken back,
                        as decided.

★

    you have sacrificed in my desire.

+

Under atmosphere blue as decided,
what is it that lives,
        spine-startled, thrilled by the Flutter-road
of Files-too-near?

★

Ear flushed of its privacies,
            flushed of its silences,
drawn out to the husband, the Breath,

as Kant walked into Beauty,
forgetting why he opened the door—

"For neither the veil nor the veiled object is the beautiful,
        but the object in its veil"—

Kant catches fire.

★

The rest is the hymn.
What you see despite the eye is the hymn.

This woman reeking of urine is the hymn.
Jean with her doll-crimped thin dyed hair is the hymn.

★

The moist cloud spits the star-seed.
      So begins the sacrifice.
The moon brings the white sheet.

Who accepts breath is sacrifice.
Who sings
      sings worlds frightened and dear.

from *Colorado Review*

Vague Poem

◇　◇　◇

The trip west
—I think I *dreamed* that trip.
They talked a lot of "rose rocks"
or maybe "rock roses"
—I'm not sure now, but someone tried to get me some.
(And two or three students had.)

She said she had some at her house.
They were by the back door, she said.
—A ramshackle house.
An Army house? No, "a *Navy* house." Yes,
that far inland.
There was nothing by the back door but dirt
or that same dry, monochrome, sepia straw I'd seen everywhere.
Oh, she said, the dog has carried them off.
(A big black dog, female, was dancing around us.)

Later, as we drank tea from mugs, she found one
"a sort of one." "This one is just beginning. See—
you can see here, it's beginning to look like a rose.
It's—well, a crystal, crystals form—
I don't know any geology myself . . ."
(Neither did I.)
Faintly, I could make out—perhaps—in the dull,
rose-red lump of (apparently) soil
a rose-like shape; faint glitters . . . Yes, perhaps
there was a secret, powerful crystal at work inside.

I *almost* saw it: turning into a rose
without any of the intervening
roots, stem, buds, and so on; just
earth to rose and back again.
Crystallography and its laws:
something I once wanted badly to study,
until I learned that it would involve a lot of arithmetic,
　　that is, mathematics.

Just now, when I saw you naked again,
I thought the same words: rose-rock, rock-rose . . .
Rose, trying, working, to show itself,
forming, folding over,
unimaginable connections, unseen, shining edges.
Rose-rock, unformed, flesh beginning, crystal by crystal,
clear pink breasts and darker, crystalline nipples,
rose-rock, rose-quartz, roses, roses, roses,
exacting roses from the body,
and the even darker, accurate, rose of sex—

from *The New Yorker*

The French Generals

◊   ◊   ◊

Whenever Jesus appears at the murky well,
I am there with my five hundred husbands.
It takes Jesus all day to mention their names.

The growing soul longs for mastery, but
The small men inside pull it into misery.
It is the nature of shame to have many children.

Earth's name is "Abundance of Desires." The serpent
Sends out his split tongue and waves it
In the air scented with so many dark Napoleons.

A general ends his life in a small cottage
With damp sheets and useless French franc notes;
He keeps his plans of attack under the mattress.

I have said to the serpent: "This is your house."
I bring in newspapers to make his nest cozy.
It's the nature of wanting to have many wives.

Sturdy rafters in lifejackets are pulled down
Till their toes touch the bottom of the Rogue River.
Wherever there is water there is someone drowning.

from *The Paris Review*

LEE ANN BROWN

Sonnet Around Stephanie

◊   ◊   ◊

What rituals are in Benares?
Our little cat's grave smells of incense, earth—
three candles, three days now, burning.
Through the window from my desk I can see

them in the dark. Beneath yellow leaves
is the earth we all pressed down, turning
it over to smell it dark with ferns.
His spirit plays in shadow, we still see

it in the halls. In my mind, your self-portrait
slowly unwraps suicidal arms to show your face.
Blessed are the small, for they shall be buried.

Blown into darkness, I could only wait
for the Gift to come around again—drawn to empty space.
Blessed are the angry, for they shall be carried.

from *Verse*

Notes About My Face

◇ ◇ ◇

1
Traces. Then things themselves are not names
not words only.

2
Hay. I am not hay.
I am not hey either.
My mother meant one of these. Or both.

3
Both moons in one month.
Both rains on Tuesday.
Both cold snows on 5.

4
Reaching for the salt:
a) she is stabbed by the father
b) she is stabbed by the father's fork
c) she is stabbed by the father's father
d) hello. she is inside

5
"I miss myself
in the earlier version"
I write to Jean.

6
"interesting"—1 of my mask words

7
she is inside:
                    "I" wrote

to literal companion of
mine in literal light
on "porch-stage" (Jean's)
of 1968, the summer the

New Yorker published a
translation by Babel's daughter
of "You Must Know Everything"
—and Jane Flory read it

aloud in the back evening
—and Sheldon Flory took
notes about my face during
this and put them in a

                    poem—
                    or so
                    it
                    seems

then—Jean Valentine's small
"porch-stage . . ."
"ghost guide . . ."
i became "I" at some pivot
in this place —> arrow
                    is the
                    face of,
face of

No rearranged rider.
No ghost behaviors.
No umbrella.

8
"too much glass" K's
translation of T reads
—one thinks of one's own
house or house past or
room as having too much
too—but one is silent

no recovery artist
no box of recovery
the boys in the basement
are shattered in the skull
and in the heart—in the
cases

9
of these two murders by
the father the heart is
equal in size to the shattered
skull and the shattered window

10
and in at least 6 other moments
on this globe this appropriate word
globe for this earth at at least
6 other moments there are equal
murders—the word daily cannot
convey this—the broken branch
on 16th Street two Novembers ago
is the link to the moment of one
of the two deaths

11
your honor
my thesis will be based
upon Myung Mi Kim's DURA
and Duras' Two by Duras
The Atlantic Man
The Slut of the Normandy Coast
a new world

12
how to refer to these two (Two)
will be the initial pivot
and probably final pivot
feeble insomnia
brick of the school

13
the elementary school
in e elementary evening

14
something like candy cities
—"*Waipo* stands for maternal grandma. *Wai* means "outside,"
"stranger." *Po,* "old woman."   (Wang Ping,"Female Marriage")

I want my Maypo.
outside means no snow
outside means stolen drawing from snow's friend
outside means Jean Valentine's "ghost guide"

15
I had this feeling
                              Sheldon was up
to something, Jane too—

maybe not Jane, maybe not Jean
—sometimes, from Jean's incredible
poem Ironwood

sometimes I thought I was
"the other Michael"—
                              I asked her
last November, finally,
after wanting to ask for

a long time, and she sort
of said she could not recall
who that was—were we walking
along arm in arm

after she gives this wonderful
reading of poems from this
book she is now thinking (May)

of calling HER LOST BOOK.
I don't believe her, about "the other
Michael," but it becomes vague now

like a snowy fact, like some of
the most interesting facts in poems
do—mask facts

literal light:

16
LAMB
  | cuban
  | panther
JASPER JOHNS—ANXIETY—A MAN WHO WANTED ME BUT I WAS
      WRONG
Street of pain
Someone is actually going to pay me to hang out in churches
"I don't want an adversarial relationship c̄ my writing, you have"
Don't sleep with your head in the sun here
"I COME FROM SECRETS" John Frazier
have told our dog a dog we had another dog we had a story we should not
LATIN "His friends did not see him for months."
too much house too much wind in the sense of wind against trees and house
The liability of the inside
Kim's "Large pond gives way"
Kim's Collect the years' duration
"AND YEARS AGO, TOO"   Melissa Hotchkiss   Could *not* see the ball
      coming
said his brother, and the rain helped the silent father understand his silence
again: the songs
little did you know i almost threw myself under the train tonight
little did you know
people claim people like objects
today the story of my friend the sea. Tomorrow, utter sexuality of the sea
YOU PROBABLY WON'T STEAL FROM YOUR MOTHER IN LAW

AGAIN FOR AWHILE

i was intimidated by weldon kees
painted digression 8500 ghosts today painted senators with money bags for
     faces
painted representatives with blades for ears painted soldiers with assholes
for brains painted murderers with US painted all over their hearing
painted punishments for another woman   painted brutality for another
     child
evening coast loan sudden reverse far scamper duck globe refrain to per
     drop
see my difficult gone he talked part door she broughtnightly crows
this bird was a sign or not unhate the hand the pelvis   hello blue moon

from *American Poetry Review*

Heartland

◇　◇　◇

And she saying, I cannot quite
hear what she says, but he, standing
in clothes washed too often still
to be warm, looks out at the land.

And she saying, I cannot hear
what follows his name, and he, "What's
it all meant, Lizzie? We've made
a living and no one doubts our name."

And he remembering the years
before the green combines and long,
open barns for machinery
and their hands on each other young.

And she saying, I cannot tell
whether or not it's comforting,
until he turns to a door that
is not a new house and goes in.

And she saying, I can hear now,
"If the words are old, let them be.
It's hard enough with a dream;
here, what can you see of a plan?"

And he nodding, I can no longer
hear what she says, the house shadowed

by combines and long open barns,
the fields planted and bare for rain.

from *The Nation*

Blouse of Felt

◇　◇　◇

Assembly tree and bowl of thorns
     You see these hanging vases we have flogged
Hooded bell saved, illustrations in
black on green, the Admirable clutched at his lapel
as I touched him
    thistle and all—organized by
a monk in spike breeches
of assurance these four-pointed stars aren't upset
       or a tad fish with savior heart—
      nettles imprinted

Pinwheel caught in the stillness of cremation
Spikes wedded, bathed umbrella

My collar holds a ball, mitts bulb-ended

    Capital of magnified balsam, the
plot opening season-burst
Someone has burned these poles!
Carted away my polestars!

Christmas is a Japanese hour   these barlamps
    of clay arranged
such that   to decipher their lay one must
be embalmed in a necklace of paperwhites

      Shoot moon-bleached, crush scattered
near garden's plump seizure

All the spiked blades of a flung disc   *and*
whirling at the center is a pom-pom
that spills its shadow   into this evening

        for the Admirable assures me
armed with unfolding cabbages,
lilac javelin, and glockenbud

        they can view us from the square portals atop
the nut-shaped hill itself balanced upon a stalk
        Poppy vent, or the signs of a
        mineral fall pulling sleep first

Three looking away, one begging to be penetrated
or the corolla of an albino dune-flower

What is that . . .?
        —a perpetrator I found on my widower's mat

A white fever of tiger, cut by   Omen's shards,

tunnel babble, and weathered
the advancement of quickened speech—
        floral listening

        In one frame his hand reaches to pluck a raisin's past
        In the next our cheeks are at the bottom
        of a glaze toward his wall of tan and russet
        In the last a ferret has gone limp on his lip

A leaf then grew to house
the faint creature—oranges
secretly ripened as he nursed its
Prussian health

From *Faucheuse*

Longing, a documentary

◇ ◇ ◇

Shot List

1. Night.
    River.

    subtitle: *It was for such a night she had waited.*

2. Trunk of her car is open and lit by a funnel of light from the porch.

3. She loads the trunk: 4x6 trays, photographic papers, strobe light.
    Strobe doesn't fit, she angles it into the backseat.

4. She is driving, concentrating, empty highway.

    subtitle: *She was not a person who aimed at eventual*
    reconciliation with the views of common sense.

5. She is at the river in deep reeds, watching.

6. She wades along the edge of the river, watching.

7. Night plucks her, she stumbles, stops.

8. She is bending beside the car, unpacking trays.

9. She drags the trays through deep reeds toward the river.
    Moon unclouds itself and plunges by.

Night is not a fact.

10. She walks into the river.

Facts lack something, she thought.

11. She positions the big trays on the riverbottom near the bank, just under the water, spreads photographic papers in them, adjusts it, moves back. Watches.

12. She stands by the strobe in deep reeds.

13. Flash of strobe surprises the riverbank.

14. She sits awhile in the reeds, arms on knees.

"Overtakelessness" (what facts lack).

15. Moonlight sways down through black water onto the photographic papers.

16. She is driving, windows blowing, empty highway.

As usual she enjoyed the sense of work, of having worked. Other fears would soon return.

from *The Threepenny Review*

Ceriserie

◇ ◇ ◇

Music: Sexual misery is wearing you out.

Music: Known as the Philosopher's Stair for the world-weariness which climbing it inspires. One gets nowhere with it.

Paris: St-Sulpice in shrouds.

Paris: You're falling into disrepair, Eiffel Tower this means you! Swathed in gold paint, Enguerrand Quarton whispering come with me under the shadow of this gold leaf.

Music: The unless of a certain series.

Mathematics: Everyone rolling dice and flinging Fibonacci, going to the opera, counting everything.

Fire: The number between four and five.

Gold leaf: Wedding dress of the verb *to have,* it reminds you of of.

Music: As the sleep of the just. We pass into it and out again without seeming to move. The false motion of the wave, "frei aber einsam."

Steve Evans: I saw your skull! It was between your thought and your face.

Melisse: How I saw her naked in Brooklyn but was not in Brooklyn at the time.

Art: That's the problem with art.

Paris: I was in Paris at the time! St-Sulpice in shrouds "like Katharine Hepburn."

Katharine Hepburn: Oh America! But then, writing from Paris in the thirties, it was to you Benjamin compared Adorno's wife. Ghost citizens of the century, sexual misery is wearing you out.

Misreading: You are entering the City of Praise, population two million three-hundred thousand . . .

Hausmann's Paris: The daughter of Midas in the moment just after. The first silence of the century then the king weeping.

Music: As something to be inside of, as inside thinking one feels thought of, fly in the ointment of the mind!

Sign at Jardin des Plantes: GAMES ARE FORBIDDEN IN THE LABYRINTH.

Paris: Museum city, gold lettering the windows of the wedding-dress shops in the Jewish Quarter. "Nothing has been changed," sez Michael, "except for the removal of twenty-seven thousand Jews."

Paris 1968: The anti-museum museum.

The Institute for Temporary Design: Scaffolding, traffic jam, barricade, police car on fire, flies in the ointment of the city.

Gilles Ivain: In your tiny room behind the clock, your bent sleep, your Mythomania.

Gilles Ivain: Our hero, our Anti-Hausmann.

To say about Flemish painting: "Money-colored light."

Music: "Boys On The Radio."

Boys of the Marais: In your leather pants and sexual pose, arcaded shadows of the Place des Vosges.

Mathematics: And all that motion you supposed was drift, courtyard with the grotesque head of Apollinaire, Norma on the bridge, proved nothing but a triangle fixed by the museum and the opera and St-Sulpice in shrouds.

The Louvre: A couple necking in an alcove, in their brief bodies entwined near the Super-Radiance Hall visible as speech.

Speech: The bird that bursts from the mouth shall not return.

Pop song: We got your pretty girls they're talking on mobile phones la la la.

Enguerrand Quarton: In your dream gold leaf was the sun, salve on the kingdom of the the visible.

Gold leaf: The mind makes itself a Midas, it cannot hold and not have.

Thus: I came to the city of possession.

Sleeping: Behind the clock, in the diagon, in your endless summer night, in the city remarking itself like a wave in which people live or are said to live, it comes down to the same thing, an exaggerated sense of things getting done.

Paris: The train station's a museum, opera in the place of the prison.

Later: The music lacquered with listen.

from *American Poetry Review*

Snow Day

◇　◇　◇

Today we woke up to a revolution of snow,
its white flag waving over everything,
the landscape vanished,
not a single mouse to punctuate the blankness,
and beyond these windows

the government buildings smothered,
schools and libraries buried, the post office lost
under the noiseless drift,
the paths of trains softly blocked,
the world fallen under this falling.

In a while, I will put on some boots
and step out like someone walking in water,
and the dog will porpoise through the drifts,
and I will shake a laden branch
sending a cold shower down on us both.

But for now I am a willing prisoner in this house,
a sympathizer with the anarchic cause of snow.
I will make a pot of tea
and listen to the plastic radio on the counter,
as glad as anyone to hear the news

that the Kiddie Corner School is closed,
the Ding-Dong School, closed,
the All Aboard Children's School, closed,
the Hi-Ho Nursery School, closed,
along with—some will be delighted to hear—

the Toadstool School, the Little School,
Little Sparrows Nursery School,
Little Stars Pre-School, Peas-and-Carrots Day School
the Tom Thumb Child Center, all closed,
and—clap your hands—the Peanuts Play School.

So this is where the children hide all day,
these are the nests where they letter and draw,
where they put on their bright miniature jackets,
all darting and climbing and sliding,
all but the few girls whispering by the fence.

And now I am listening hard
in the grandiose silence of the snow,
trying to hear what those three girls are plotting,
what riot is afoot,
which small queen is about to be brought down.

from *The Atlantic Monthly*

ROBERT CREELEY

En Famille

◇ ◇ ◇

I wandered lonely as a cloud . . .
I'd seemingly lost the crowd
I'd come with, family—father, mother, sister and brothers—
fact of a common blood.

Now there was no one,
just my face in the mirror, coat on a single hook,
a bed I could make getting out of.
Where had they gone?

•

What was that vague determination
cut off the nurturing relation
with all the density, this given company—
what made one feel such desperation

to get away, get far from home, be gone from those
would know us even if they only saw our noses or our toes,
accept with joy our helpless mess,
taking for granted it was part of us?

•

My friends, hands on each other's shoulders,
holding on, keeping the pledge
to be for one, for all, a securing center,
no matter up or down, or right or left—

to keep the faith, keep happy, keep together,
keep at it, so keep on
despite the fact of necessary drift.
Home might be still the happiest place on earth?

•

You won't get far by yourself.
It's dark out there.
There's a long way to go.
The dog knows.

It's him loves us most,
or seems to, in dark nights of the soul.
Keep a tight hold.
Steady, we're not lost.

•

Despite the sad vagaries,
anchored in love, placed in the circle,
young and old, a round—
love's fact of this bond.

One day one will look back
and think of them—
where they were, now gone—
remember it all.

•

Turning inside as if in dream,
the twisting face I want to be my own,
the people loved and with me still,
I see their painful faith.

Grow, dears, then fly away!
But when the dark comes, then come home.
Light's in the window, heart stays true.
Call—and I'll come to you.

•

The wind blows through the shifting trees
outside the window, over the fields below.
Emblems of growth, of older, younger,
of towering size or all the vulnerable hope

as echoes in the images of these three
look out with such reflective pleasure,
so various and close. They stand there,
waiting to hear a music they will know.

•

I like the way you both look out at me.
Somehow it's sometimes hard to be a human.
Arms and legs get often in the way,
making oneself a bulky, awkward burden.

Tell me your happiness is simply true.
Tell me I can still learn to be like you.
Tell me the truth is what we do.
Tell me that care for one another is the clue.

•

We're here because there's nowhere else to go,
we've come in faith we learned as with all else.
Someone once told us and so it is we know.
No one is left outside such simple place.

No one's too late, no one can be too soon.
We comfort one another, making room.
We dream of heaven as a climbing stair.
We look at stars and wonder why and where.

•

Have we told you all you'd thought to know?
Is it really so quickly now the time to go?

Has anything happened you will not forget?
Is where you are enough for all to share?

Is wisdom just an empty word?
Is age a time one might finally well have missed?
Must humanness be its own reward?
Is happiness this?

from *Boston Book Review*

A Mown Lawn

◇   ◇   ◇

She hated a *mown lawn*. Maybe that was because *mow* was the reverse of *wom*, the beginning of the name of what she was—a *woman*. A *mown lawn* had a sad sound to it, like a *long moan*. From her, a *mown lawn* made a *long moan*. *Lawn* had some of the letters of *man*, though the reverse of *man* would be *Nam*, a bad war. A *raw war*. *Lawn* also contained the letters of *law*. In fact, *lawn* was a contraction of *lawman*. Certainly a *lawman* could and did *mow a lawn*. *Law and order* could be seen as starting from *lawn order*, valued by so many Americans. *More lawn* could be made using a *lawn mower*. A *lawn mower* did make *more lawn*. *More lawn* was a contraction of *more lawmen*. Did *more lawn* in America make *more lawmen* in America? Did *more lawn* make *more Nam*? *More mown lawn* made *more long moan*, from her. Or a *lawn mourn*. So often, she said, Americans wanted *more mown lawn*. All of America might be one *long mown lawn*. A *lawn* not *mown* grows *long*, she said: better a *long lawn*. Better a *long lawn* and a *mole*. Let the *lawman* have the *mown lawn*, she said. Or the *moron*, the *lawn moron*.

from *McSweeney's Quarterly*

Ma Ramon

◇   ◇   ◇

Ma Ramon would fall upon the floor
feigning death at her children's no's
when they were too grown to force the bending

M' pa palé anglé, she'd say, *no eenglees*
to tax collectors and those too dark to fall
within her notice. She a grand lady
of Abercrombie Street now the capital
was under the Queen and not the rusted
Republique. She did not
believe in London, the pappy show
that was the civil service, good jobs
for brown faces behind a desk.

She believed in land. Her own mystical origins
lay *en la France,* in red-haired green-eyed
aristocrats escaping *guillotines* and *egalité*
for seven mountains they would call their own
and though she had to marry black for money
she never forgot she was person of *qualité.*

She kept her parchment mother in lace and linen
photographed herself with all her siblings
maintained a piano in the parlor
for butter-skinned suitors with Creole tongues
to swirl the Castilian with dervish daughters
petticoats twining with worsted knickers.

Eh ben, Lucretia, *Allé* Ena, *Oú ça* John
Vini Vivi, *Dansé, dansé, li beau, nuh?*
Mes belles enfants, my beautiful cream children.

from *Callaloo*

The Cloud of Unknowing

◇ ◇ ◇

Is not a cloud at all
But a wall colored so efficiently
It seems to be an alley of trees
Some believe this cul de sac
Can be approached from every angle
While others consider it merely a frontage road
To remnants of summer, a disused
Anchorage inside the spiral jetty. But we
Have seen this cloud, you and I have,
Just before we set out to martinize the infidel
It was there, somewhere in the Sahara,
Hovering above an Italian restaurant
Perched on the edge of a depression. White-tunicked
Waiters with jet-black hair served us cannelloni
And Chianti yet at the same time did not
Serve us cannelloni and Chianti—but then
We were at sea as we always were in those days
On a ferry yes the Dover ferry
Everyone was heaving
Patches of sawdust everywhere on deck
Always followed by the cloud
The sun came out but it was still raining
North of Leningrad the tramline ends
We trudge through acres of mud between
Grim apartment blocks in a colorless landscape
Day for night whistling in the sleet
The mud becomes woods, beyond the woods
We finally reach the little wooden village on the far side of a hill—
Bent-bark roofs as in the poem—

With a little Orthodox church, a bit like St-Cloud
From a distance this is Old Russia I think
We meet the priest whom I like
Immediately we parted as old friends—
Never saw him again. Funny, like the
Facial expressions of the father-and-son
Pickpocket team in the Mexico City subway
June rush hour you all of a sudden turn to
Shake their hands *"¡Que pasa?!"* They looked
As if they had seen a ghost
Probably like my own face when I lost my passport
In a dream. I was in Heathrow and hung my coat
On the convenient too convenient rack outside the duty-free shops
The Pakistani woman at the gate was very helpful
But could not help me. For some reason
I was interested only in which languages she spoke
The truth was all I wanted was for her
To say Urdu, which she did.

from *Boston Review*

THOMAS SAYERS ELLIS

T.A.P.O.A.F.O.M.

(The Awesome Power of a Fully-Operational Memory)

◇   ◇   ◇

for Sharan Strange

1 ALIENATION

The cassette tape
you sent had a sloppy,
secret second coming on it,
not to mention

the magic-markered mugs
of afronauts
with new spaceships
not manufactured

up south
in any of those privately-owned,
aspirin-white ghettos
ringworming the ozone.

Thanks! You've been here.
You know what
artist colonization is like:
lunchmeataphobia

and black radioinactive levels
of love amnesia
dense as the cosmos.
A brotherloadless UFO.

Only me and Michael S. Harper.
Barely a sister either,
except Afro-Sappho:
Sapphire.

        All of one
day-one month
in the supergroovalistic guerrilla
Nipple Room
and nothing computes.

No wonder they call it Yaddo.
After Faber and Faber
it's the whitest, most minus-da-groove
diaperspace I go:

icka tit,
icka clit,
icka prick,
lickety-split.

Deeper still, I didn't come here to thighlight
empty memory's bangalang mutiny
to zeep then zapp
glitter's non-linear re-entry.

2 ANNIVERSARY

July 5, 1996. Central Park,
New York City. Both mobs up-in-here,
all of their survivors
and damn-near

half ours: you, me, Vera, Major
and Gelonia as well as
a few extended inkslingers.
I ran into Darius James

(who introduced me
to Pedro Bell) and Tracie Morris,
summer-swimming the crowd.
Pump up and down.

Ah underground angel!
Ah gaps and gadgets!
A limousine arrived from Mars.
Baldass Kabbabie babbled.

Remember? It was November 22, 1986.
I was writing a paper
on Jean Vigo,
and you, Sharan, you were looking

for one of Chris Marker's
films, on video.
Ten years is not a long time
for poetry, but it is for us.

Next we were all living together in Cambridge.
After that, freeing and reading black books.
Then, precious lord, James Baldwin died
and we became a church.

Ah! Those Dark Room Sundays
and their infinite, unrehearsed, double-mouthed
                marches toward the rear.
Some readings you really could hear
a rat piss on cotton

and on off weekends
workshops equally dark and feeling.

Your eloquent *Ash* was promoted there,
        in the funkcronomix,
between memory and experience.

Memory, Walcott says, moves backwards.
If this is true, your memory is a mothership
        minus the disco-sadistic silver
all stars need to shine. Tell the world.
A positive nuisance. Da bomb.

from *AGNI*

The Art of the Snake Story

◇ ◇ ◇

I.   In Greece in 1939, these kids had this little snake trapped in a corner, kicking it and laughing. I charged in, all the hero, "Leave the snake alone," and (I was very high at the time) picked it up and took it outside. Suddenly I was in horrible pain. I looked down, and the snake had its teeth in the web of skin between my thumb and first finger, right here. I let go, and the snake just hung from my hand like some weird tumor, giving off that glandular, musky smell of ingratitude. The worst thing was, all the abominable children could see me from the door. So I had to wait until I was out of sight before thrashing my arm and screaming.

II.   He had almost made his cautious way across the waterfall. He was shaking part of a fallen tree to test if it was a solid hand rail or not. A medium-sized rattlesnake was sunning itself on a high branch, got shaken off. In the air next to his head I saw it, the flabby gun-metal body with its frightening marks making an S it was moving through, as if the ink were sliding out of the letter. The snake landed audibly. Dead leaf scramble, quite suddenly he was back on this side of the waterfall. We had the following conversation. "What was it?" "A rattler." "Was it a rattler?" "It was a rattler." "It was only a foot away from you. Are you all right?" "It ran off." "Do you want to walk some more?" "No, I don't."

III.   It's coiled on a rock on the bank, it rears up and hisses at us. I say leave it be, but Stu says no, someone else might pass by too close and not see it. So he stands up in the boat with his oar and tries to smash it. It's in the water and then in the boat, it must be six feet long, and it is *mad*. But at last it's good and dead, so we take the beer out of the cooler and coil it up in there and close the lid.

We're floating along, fishing and talking, we drift right up alongside these three old geezers fishing off a dock, and they say, you catching anything? Stu, recognizing a priceless opportunity, says, yeah, wanna see? and opens up the cooler. That cottonmouth comes shooting out of there like one of those joke snakes out of a can of nuts. Nobody gets hurt except the snake, which we have to kill all over again. Those old guys though, they don't stay and help. They pick up their lawn chairs and leave, looking unhappy with the whole world.

I suggest throwing the snake overboard this time. Stu says he has to keep it to show to his wife or she'll never believe us. So now we flop and twist it into the cooler again, and buzz back to the house. His wife says, as we come up carrying our burden, what did you catch for us, and he says, lookie here. Well, you can guess what happens next. This time, he gets bit on the ankle.

IV.   No, Felix died. I was out of town when it happened. In fact, Greg decided he would save him until he could take him to the lab and get him stripped down for the skeleton. But he didn't bother to tell me that. The day after I came back, I went through the packages in the freezer and had the shock of my life.

> Snake eternity. Because
>   Of the way biting its tail made a circle.
>   We're in Hall C,
>   An illustration, c, of
>   How no snake really did this.
>   Never rolled downhill
>   As a wheel, never bit off
>   Its own ending.
>   Or: you have heard
>   Of the Gnostic snake? Wisdom-Jesus as a
>   Serpent convinced
>   The two to know.
>   There's also the quaint idea
> Snakes are the spirits of dead
> Heros (this concerns us—we
> Are a museum.) Here is
> An artist's rendering of the dead hero's
> Spirit as it
> Might have landed
> On Matthew's head.

What are the elements of
  A successful snake story?
    A: **The snake must**
      Seem animate. The speaker
        Need not describe,
          Because the listener cannot help but see,
            That oblique, that
              Movement of head sideways to
                Go forward. You understand how
                  This violates the rules for
                    Artful language; the speaker
                  Cannot overestimate
                    Associations an audience brings to
                  This occasion.
              If the snake is not alive,
            The teller must
          Have thought it was. A stuffed or
        Frozen snake need not detract
      From the story. And notice
    How the word gun-
  Metal is used
Twice—surely significant.

V.   This last time I talked to Alice—Alice had been really depressed lately, what with trying to finish her thesis and all, but this last time I called she had just bought this snake and was all excited. It got kind of boring to listen to, actually—my snake this, my snake that. Well. She called me today in tears: the snake crawled into her computer. She can't turn it on now, for fear of, you know, electrocuting him? She knows he's in there because she blew some cigarette smoke into the opening, and he stuck his nose out for a second. He hasn't eaten for a long time, and she can't write her thesis without her computer, and what is she going to *do*? I mean, this is getting too weird. I mean this snake thing. Why didn't she get a hamster or something.

VI.   According to the Bangkok guidebook, they milked the cobras at the cobra farm every day at two. But when I got there, the time had been changed to twelve, and I had missed the whole thing.

Checkout Receipt

Central Library: Santa Rosa
01/26/11 12:55PM

****

Borrower Number: 212783

Julie & Julia
37565050945770 ------------- 02/02/11
Easy rider
37565050356960 ------------- 02/02/11
Scoop
37565050673644 ------------- 02/02/11
Manhattan
37565050351608 ------------- 02/02/11
The Best American car poetry, 2001 /
10006473063-3 ------------- 02/16/11

TOTAL: 5

For account information, review items
being held, renew items, & more!!!
TELL-IC DIAL-IN 566-0281
www.sonomalibrary.org

VII.   I was working in the garden, and I almost tripped over a rattlesnake. I called pest control, and they were pretty condescending. They said it was probably a hog snake and that hog snakes were *good*. An hour later I called back and said that I had the hog snake trapped in a garbage can, where it was making distinctive rattling noises. They came out and killed it for me, and they were much more polite.

They said to cut the head off, throw the body away, and bury the head carefully so that it wouldn't be dug up again. It sounds like voodoo, but I guess the poison doesn't decay, and water can reconstitute it, and you can walk on it and absorb it right through your skin.

VIII.   This was back in Bombay when I was, oh, a very young boy. I was strictly forbidden to go into the attic, so of course when I found the door unlocked one day, I started up at once.

My friend, it was very dark. There was no electricity in the attic. But there was just enough daylight to make out an enormous cobra right in front of me, ready to strike. I froze. The cobra did not move. The cobra and I remained this way for about half an hour—the stuffed cobra, as it turned out.

IX.   This was when we, my family, lived in Michigan. We had a lot of barn cats, and it used to be my job to go out and fill a bucket with water for them. I had to refill it every day in the winter, because it would freeze over. So I went out to the barn and grabbed the bucket. I'd only taken a few steps when I knew that the weight was off somehow. I looked down, and there was a bronze snake coiled around the outside of the bucket. Evidently it had chosen this spot when it was warmer, and it was now frozen in place. To tell the truth, I never found out if it was alive or not. I screamed, threw the bucket down, and ran into the house. My mother came out with a hoe and chopped it into twenty pieces—strange. Why can't you just chop the thing in half and stop? It doesn't ever seem like a snake is dead enough, does it.

B: **The snake must**
Startle. These are
With one exception stories
    About not expecting snakes.
        Alice, for example, did
          Not really think

The snake would be
In the computer; she only looked because
She had been unsuccessful
Looking elsewhere.
For a brief moment when she
Saw the snake's nose, she even
Thought, "Snake!" before
Remembering it was a snake she wished to find
C: **There must have actually been a snake.**
Grossest exaggeration,
While permissible, is not
Necessary.
Enough, if it
Is true, to say,
"I saw." No lie
Is more hideous than the
Invented snake encounter.
This belongs to (line up along the right, please)
An oral tradition. This word, said with a
Specific register of urgency is
Last bastion of
Word equals thing. You can see a squiggled line
In the raconteur's pupil.
More than that, the snake teller, perpetrating
Horrors, *becomes* a snake, like
Christabel's hiss—
Becomes, and you
Become him, or her, frozen.
These are not in fact stories,
But frames for the one instant,
When a blowing vine, dead stick
Vertiginously metamorphoses, oh,
Sickening, into something living. D: **The
Story reminds
You that anything at any time may be-
Come snake.** We petrify to
Make up for it.

X.   They have these little brown snakes there, no longer than that.
They like to coil up inside of flowers. You go to smell this pretty flower
and you die. Also these giant spiders, this gun-metal blue-black color,
like to build their webs across the trail. They kill you too. I tell you, I
was a hell of a lot more scared of the wildlife then I ever was of the
enemy.

This last was overheard by
          A herpetologist on
                A train. She managed to photograph it: Here
                      Is the perpetrator. You can just tell what
                            His friends call him, him with his
                            Tale in his mouth.

          from *Quarter After Eight*

Contemporary American Poetry

◇   ◇   ◇

Maybe when her eye first gave her trouble, but when I did not yet know
This was a growth that would spread through her brain, Mother sent me
Donald Hall's "Kicking the Leaves," which she'd torn from the *Times,*

One of the clippings that piled up around her feet while she read
To scout out the news for half-a-dozen people,
But particularly for her children, particularly for me.

Hall—so uncool—in a poem so humble and conventional,
Where the leaves are dying leaves, not pie plates,
And stand for what we always know they stand for.

In a way, this poem was my mother's leave-taking,
What she would have said to me if she wrote poems.
My darling, she tried to say, through Hall's poem,

I will soon be leaving you. When you hear about my death
You will be staring at a blood red leaf against a raw blue
October sky through a film of tears, and you will be

An orphan. The price you will have to pay
For having been loved—essentially without qualification—
By me. I am leaving you now with this clipping,

This poem about leaves from the editorial page of the Times,
Which I read daily, always with thoughts of you.
How I resented this poem, which moved me terribly,

Though it was completely without jokes or irony,
Unadorned and sad as a New England graveyard,
The anthem of our family, not designed for tragedy,

Other than the loss of each other, my mother signaling to me
Through the voice of her bearded Protestant avatar.
I diminish, not them, as I go first into the leaves

Taking the step they will follow, Octobers and years from now.
Mother, you'd be eighty-four, though younger than some of my students.
Like them, you'd listen skeptically to my praise for my contemporaries

Like Louise Glück. *Her mother, Bea, went to high school with me*
In the Twenties. She's added the umlaut. Remember
Her paintings at the library when she just got out of the hospital?

See, dear, you were never troubled or gloomy enough to be a poet,
Though, like Donald Hall, you have and will have losses.
Remember his poem about the leaves? I sent you a clipping once,

Though I know you always threw out my clippings.
Still, I sent them, messages for you piling up around my feet
Each night as I sat and read the Times *and thought of you.*

Now the poem's in our *Contemporary American Poetry* anthology,
One that puts old enemies, like O'Hara and Lowell, together
In an academy of poetry of the world to come.

And Hall, who looks healthy now, also had cancer,
And nearly died, but here he's still in his mid-forties,
Happy his long drought is over and he's writing again.

He's kicking the leaves, leaping and exultant, recovering from death,
And I am re-reading his poem, thinking of myself at thirty,
Scornful and envious, moved and suspicious, reading in his poem,

One of the few my mother ever cared to send me,
About what he calls *the pleasure, the only long pleasure*
Of taking a place in the story of leaves, which is one hundred percent grief.

The pleasure, if there is one, is knowing we have the dead inside us,
Where they have to make peace with us, and never leave us.
My mother, in class today, though dead way back,

Will go home to hang her coat in the closet of heaven and say:
What a wonderful class! I don't like much in contemporary American poetry,
Except for "Kicking the Leaves" by Donald Hall. But the teacher—

He's like that Louis Rukeyser on "Wall $treet Week"
I watch faithfully, though I leave the investing to Barney.
A man like that—anything he says is worth listening to.

from *Poetry*

Little Dantesque

◇　◇　◇

It turns out
The dogs were in control all along.

Hard by the hinges of hell—
A faculty party.

Everyone drifts
In their disastrous bodies.

Sudden furniture,
A hint of eucalyptus.

Someone plugs in the flowers.

1.
I've been a has-been.
Now I'm a was. I was
Promoted.

2.
The dogs were in control all along.
They saw everything.

3.
I had a happy medium—
Had her reading out of my palm.
The circus folded up and left—

A riot of life forms
And annoying colors whisked
Like bright scarves up a sleeve.

4.
The dogs want out.
How like them.

from *Fence*

Time

◇   ◇   ◇

There was too much, always, then too little.
Childhood: sickness.
By the side of the bed I had a little bell—
at the other end of the bell, my mother.

Sickness, gray rain. The dogs slept through it. They slept on the bed,
at the end of it, and it seemed to me they understood
about childhood: best to remain unconscious.

The rain made gray slats on the windows.
I sat with my book, the little bell beside me.
Without hearing a voice, I apprenticed myself to a voice.
Without seeing any sign of the spirit, I determined
to live in the spirit.

The rain faded in and out.
Month after month, in the space of a day.
Things became dreams; dreams became things.

Then I was well; the bell went back to the cupboard.
The rain ended. The dogs stood at the door,
panting to go outside.

I was well, then I was an adult.
And time went on—it was like the rain,
so much, so much, as though it was a weight that couldn't be moved.

I was a child, half sleeping.
I was sick; I was protected.

And I lived in the world of the spirit,
the world of the gray rain,
the lost, the remembered.

Then suddenly the sun was shining.
And time went on, even when there was almost none left.
And the perceived became the remembered,
the remembered, the perceived.

from *The New Yorker*

My Chakabuku Mama

a comic tale

◇ ◇ ◇

My first big love was cosmically correct:
vegetarian chili, herbal tea, feng shui.

I pretended to comprehend numerology,
graphology, phrenology and the phases of the moon.

We meditated on celestial seasonings about who
should do the laundry in an equal relationship.

I slept with my head facing north abiding a vicious draught.
My shoes sat outside the door crying to be let in.

We searched together for the higher ground
through macrobiotic bushes and abstinence.

I peered into her thick transcendental glasses.
She faced the way of the Wicca.

We chanted to find our center
beneath an azure blue candle from Key food.

We never separated without talking it all out
or allowed bad vibes to invade our space.

She made breakfast on alternate Sundays
and I gave up drinking gin.

We went on camping trips every Spring.
I read dense poets and kept copious journals.

I sprinkled a pinch of salt in the four corners of each room,
and loaned all of my favorite clothes to mere acquaintances.

I never eavesdropped when she talked on the phone.
I ate fresh fruit and only argued with Con Edison.

I cut my finger nails. We played kalimba duets.
I threw out my Salems. She threw out the roach spray.

We shuddered in unison at the mention
of french fries or Table Talk pies.

I never watched TV
or listened to James Brown.

I gave up aspirin and wore 100% cotton,
had my tarot read, meditated on a tatami bed.

I learned to love brown rice and Japanese slippers,
eat raw fish and burn patchouli.

She could squeeze the names of three
Egyptian goddesses into any general conversation.

Malice and jealousy beat a hasty retreat. Our life moved forth
on a path of righteous awareness and sisterhood.

Then she left me flat. Exiting serenely
on a cloud of universal love.

from *Callaloo*

Gulls

◇　◇　◇

Those neck-pointing out full bodylength and calling
outwards over the breaking waves.
Those standing in waves and letting them come and
　　　　　　　　　　　　go over them.
Those gathering head-down and over some one
　　　　　　　　　　　　　　thing.
Those still out there where motion is
primarily a pulsing from underneath
and the forward-motion so slight they lay
their stillness on its swelling and falling
and let themselves swell, fall . . .
Sometimes the whole flock rising and running just
as the last film of darkness rises
leaving behind, also rising and falling in
　　　　　　　　　　tiny upliftings,
almost a mile of white underfeathers, up-turned, white spines
　　　　　　　　　　　　gliding over the wet
sand, in gusts, being blown down towards
　　　　　　　the unified inrolling awayness
　　　　　　　of white. All things turning white through
breaking. The long red pointing of lowering sun
going down on (but also streaking in towards) whoever
might be standing at the point-of-view place
from which this watching. This watching being risen
from: as glance: along the red
blurring and swaying water-path:
to the singular redness: the glance a
being-everywhere-risen-from: everywhere
cawing, mewing, cries where a

single bird lifts heavily
just at shoreline, rip where
its wing-tips (both) lap
backwash, feet still in
the wave-drag of it, to coast
on top of its own shadow and then down to not
landing.

*

Also just under the wave a thickening where
sun breaks into two red circles upon the
                    carried frothing—
white and roiling, yes, yet unbreakably red—red pushed (slicked) under
                    each wave (tucked) and, although breaking, always
                    one—(as if from the back-end-of-distance red)—
and that *one* flowing to here to
slap the red it carries in glisten-sheets
up onto shore and (also as if *onto*)
my feet.

*

[Or onto my feet, then into my eyes] where red turns into "sun" again.
So then it's sun in surf-breaking water: incircling, smearing: mind not
knowing if it's still "wave," breaking on
itself, small glider, or if it's "amidst" (red turning feathery)
or rather "over" (the laciness of foambreak) or just *what*—(among
the line of also smearingly reddening terns floating out now
on the feathery backedge of foambroken
looking)—*it is.*

*

The wind swallows my words one
                    by
one. The words leaping too, over their own
                    staying.
Oceanward too, as if being taken
                    away

92

into splash—my clutch of
                words
swaying and stemming from my
                saying, no
echo. No stopping on the temporarily exposed and drying rock
                                        out there
to rub or rest where nothing else
                grows.
And truly swift over the sands.
As if most afraid of being re-
                peated.
Preferring to be dissolved to
                designation,
backglancing stirrings,
wedged-in between unsaying and
                forgetting—
what an enterprise—spoken out by
                me as if
to *still* some last place, place becoming even as I speak
                        unspeakable—
and so punctually—not even burnt
by their crossing through the one great
                inwardness of
mind, not by the straining to be held (grasped) by my
                        meanings:
"We shall have early fruit
this year" one of the shades along the way
                calls out,
and "from the beginning" (yet further on). Words: always face-down:
listening falling upon them (as if from
                above):
listening greedy, able to put them to death,
flinging itself upon them: them open and attached
                so hard to
                what they carry:
the only evidence in them of having
                been.
And yet how they want to see behind themselves,
                as if there is something
back there, always, behind these rows I

                    gnaw the open with,
feeling them rush a bit and crane to see beneath themselves,
and always with such pain, just after emerging,
twisting on their stems to see behind, as if there were a
                                        sun
back there they need, as if it's a betrayal,
this single forward-facing: reference: dream of: ad-
                                mission: re
semblance: turning away from the page as if turning to a tryst:
the gazing-straight up at the reader there filled with ultimate
                                        fatigue:
devoted servants: road signs: footprints: you are not alone:
slowly in the listener the prisoners emerge:
slowly in you reader they stand like madmen facing into the wind:
nowhere is there any trace of blood
spilled in the service of kings, or love, or for the sake of honor,
or for some other reason.

            from *Conjunctions*

LINDA GREGERSON

Waterborne

◊ ◊ ◊

1.

The river is largely implicit here, but part
                of what
        becomes it runs from east to west beside

our acre of buckthorn and elm.
                (And part
        of that, which rather weighs on Steven's mind,

appears to have found its way to the basement. Water
                will outwit
        a wall.) It spawns real toads, our little

creek, and widens to a wetland just
                across
        the road, where shelter the newborn

fawns in May. So west among the trafficked fields,
                then south, then
        east, to join the ample Huron on its

curve beneath a one-lane bridge. This bridge
                lacks every
        grace but one, and that a sort of throwback

space for courteous digression:
                your turn,
        mine, no matter how late we are, even

the county engineers were forced to take their road
　　　　　off plumb. It's heartening
　　　to think a river makes some difference.

2.

Apart from all the difference in the world,
　　　　　that is.
　　　We found my uncle Gordon on the marsh

one day, surveying his new ditch and raining
　　　　　innovative
　　　curses on the DNR. That's Damn Near

Russia, since you ask. Apparently
　　　　　my uncle
　　　and the state had had a mild dispute, his

drainage scheme offending some considered
　　　　　larger
　　　view. His view was that the state could come

and plant the corn itself if it so loved
　　　　　spring mud. The river
　　　takes its own back, we can barely

reckon fast and slow. When Gordon was a boy
　　　　　they used to load
　　　the frozen river on a sledge here and

in August eat the heavenly reward—sweet
　　　　　cream—
　　　of winter's work. A piece of moonlight saved

against the day, he thought. And this is where
　　　　　the Muir boy
　　　drowned. And this is where I didn't.

3.

Turning of the season, and the counter-
        turn
           from ever-longer darkness into light,

and look: the river lifts to its lover the sun
           in eddying
           layers of mist as though

we hadn't irreparably fouled the planet
           after all.
           My neighbor's favorite spot for bass is just

below the sign that makes his fishing
           rod illegal,
           you might almost say the sign is half

the point. The vapors draft their languorous ex-
           curses on
           a liquid page. Better than the moment is

the one it has in mind.

from *The Atlantic Monthly*

LINDA GREGG

The Singers Change, The Music Goes On

◊ ◊ ◊

No one really dies in the myths.
No world is lost in the stories.
Everything is lost in the retelling,
in being wondered at. We grow up
and grow old in our land of grass
and blood moons, birth and goneness.
A place of absolutes. Of returning.
We live our myth in the recurrence,
pretending we will return another day.
Like the morning coming every morning.
The truth is we come back as a choir.
Otherwise Eurydice would be forever
in the dark. Our singing brings her
back. Our dying keeps her alive.

from *AGNI*

ALLEN GROSSMAN

Enough rain for Agnes Walquist

(five little fits of tears)

◇ ◇ ◇

We are all given something precious that we lose irrevocably.
—Caproni

1.

It happened at midnight.
—What I possessed and lost
or what I never possessed
and have nonetheless lost,
or what in any case I
was not born possessing
but received from another's mouth:
—a smooth stone
passed in a kiss from the mouth
of a Fate into my open mouth
amidst odors of metal
and slamming doors
at the dark end of a railway car
as the train was leaning
on a curve and slowing
to stop—is lost. Lost
in that dark!—*Dilectissima,*
the Fate showed me two ways,
male and female. Also a third:
Gessert's midnight path
to the wild *iris,*
an escaped garden among

thickets of poison oak
where rolls the stony Oregon
and hears no sound
except stone on stone.

2.

What, then, shall I give YOU?
My kiss-stone is lost.
But look! The vast world,
energetic and empty,
glows in the dark.
On the strip between the road
—gravel or macadam,
or an earthen path
(but in this case gravel)
and the settlement
or the side-hill field or forest
or other tangled right of way
for jews, gypsies, ghosts
(outcasts in any case)
there among weeds
springs up Gessert's
wild *iris tenax,* violet or pale yellow,
the bloom 3" to 5" across.
Gessert asks, "How in the world
did they come here?"
Then he says, "If you must
take these *iris,*
use a shovel. Root them
in your garden
and let them go to seed.
Gather the seed
in Fall
—October or November.
Drive out into the countryside.
Plant the seeds
on any half-sunny,
slightly eroded, roadside bank.

3.

Sow Gessert's *iris, dilectissima,*
Violet or ghostly yellow,
in the wild, universal garden
named "Shadowy Agnes Walquist,"
her midnight body
from which wild *iris*
and lilies grow.
To whom better entrust
pure loss?
To what breasts other
than the breasts
of Agnes Walquist!
—"Agnes! (Can you hear?)
when a man dies,
or a woman dies,
the whole world of which
he is the only subject
dies without residue
(or the whole world of which
she is the only subject
dies without residue).
'DID I EVER LIVE?'
'NEVER, NEVER.'
The world of each person,
man or woman,
is a dependency of the world
of another one.
When a man dies or a woman
the reason for confidence
with respect to any world
is diminished. (Weep! Weep!)
When the last person but one
dies, the last person,
though he continue to live,
ceases to exist!"
Agnes Walquist sighs.
Then she says,
YES!

4.

In my sleep I say, "Agnes! I will
give you rain
from my mystery store
of rain. The dead have buried
the dead and are forever
burying the dead.
But the dead do not remember
as the living do not know
the heart." I wake
in the hour before dawn
to the huge hammer of the rain
(hammer of sex
as the poet makes it)
which thunders enough, enough, enough."
Earth shudders and springs.
The East grows bright.
And Agnes Walquist whispers,
"Thank you."

5.

Sweet youth, sweet youth
(*dilectissima mea*)
go!
Punish thy pillow.
Your kiss-stone is among the stones
the stony Oregon rolls
and hears no sound
but stone on stone.
Blond Fate, the honey-blond,
no longer knows which one
is the stone of witness.
What follows is the wearing
out to dust.
The water mill deep down
in ocean grinds out salt
(truth, troth, death).

But sweeter than the body
of a man or a woman
(sweetness of that sweetness,
song of all those songs)
is the midnight garden
of Agnes Walquist.
Her breasts are sweet.
The huge hammer is an ancient memory
of water falling into water.
There is lightning all night
on distant mountains,
strike after strike
(violet, blue, red, ghostly yellow,
indigo).
And along the mountain paths,
asleep or dead,
are sprawled
nocturnal mountaineers.

from *The Southern Review*

Her Garden

◇   ◇   ◇

I let her garden go.
let it go, let it go
How can I watch the hummingbird
Hover to sip
With its beak's tip
The purple bee balm—whirring as we heard
It years ago?

The weeds rise rank and thick
let it go, let it go
Where annuals grew and burdock grows,
Where standing she
At once could see
The peony, the lily, and the rose
Rise over brick

She'd laid in patterns. Moss
let it go, let it go
Turns the bricks green, softening them
By the gray rocks
Where hollyhocks
That lofted while she lived, stem by tall stem,
Dwindle in loss.

from the *Times Literary Supplement* and *Tin House*

ANTHONY HECHT

Sarabande on Attaining the Age of Seventy-Seven

◇ ◇ ◇

The harbingers are come. See, see their mark;
White is their colour, and behold my head.

Long gone the smoke-and-pepper childhood smell
Of the smoldering immolation of the year,
Leaf-strewn in scattered grandeur where it fell,
Golden and poxed with frost, tarnished and sere.

And I myself have whitened in the weathers
Of heaped-up Januaries as they bequeath
The annual rings and wrongs that wring my withers,
Sober my thoughts, and undermine my teeth.

The dramatis personae of our lives
Dwindle and wizen; familiar boyhood shames,
The tribulations one somehow survives,
Rise smokily from propitiatory flames

Of our forgetfulness until we find
It becomes strangely easy to forgive
Even ourselves with this clouding of the mind,
This cinerous blur and smudge in which we live.

A turn, a glide, a quarter turn and bow,
The stately dance advances; these are airs

Bone-deep and numbing as I should know by now,
Diminishing the cast, like musical chairs.

from *The New Yorker*

Nights

◊   ◊   ◊

Ooooh, oooooh, ooooh, says the voice of a girl:

I've been attacked by owls,
by owls with towels,
I've been attacked
by snakes with rakes.

    It is just this kind of ridiculous language, banal but lacking even banality's pretense at relevance and sense, that I hear in my sleep; I wake, feeling irritable and depressed.

                        ★

The sadness! the injustice!
It's true I want to know, I want to look
But what is it?

                        ★

The fingers leave their owls in a calm
Sleep figures the features

Sleep speaks for the bird, the animal
For the round and the residual

Sleep soaks from experience
But why and what?

                        ★

Suddenly I remember having rescued a spider from the bathtub in the morning. I imagined that I had established rapport with my environment. I observed the spider eerily. I was in harmony with life and my times. Not only will things go on but this going on will repeat.

After all, I can vow kindness in relation to something I cannot know.

The spider, when it appears within "a range of alternatives," will be rescued—dished out of the nicked and polished porcelain tub and knocked onto the shrubbery just outside the open window.

Of course, it will not be the same spider each time but a sequence of spiders.

★

The 23rd night was very dark.
It was cold.
My eyes were drawn to the window.

I thought I saw a turtledove nesting on a waffle
Then I saw it was a rat doing something awful
But anarchy doesn't bother me now any more than it used to

I thought I saw a woman writing verses on a bottle
Then I saw it was a foot stepping on the throttle
But naturally freedom can be understood in many different ways

I thought I saw a fireman hosing down some straw
Then I saw it was a horse grazing in a draw
But it's always the case that in their struggle to survive, animate objects must
    be aided

I thought I saw a rhubarb pie sitting on the stove
Then I saw it was the tide receding from a cove
But although I have strong emotions when I watch a movie, jealousy is never
    one of them.

I thought I saw a bicyclist racing down the road
Then I saw it was a note, a message still in code
But sense is always either being raised to or lowered from the sky

★

A voice says, The ambered bed flag fills.
A voice says, This is voltage island.
A voice says, The wall past which girls wander flicks is built of baffled face bricks.

★

I saw a juxtaposition
It happened to be between an acrobat and a sense of obligation
Pure poetry
Of course there is a great difference between withering and a napping man
And flailing in relation to fossils in a stone is different from a set of dominoes
Still I don't worry less about the same old worries

★

I'm of a mule age, I dare like a log.
I live where I live, and I'll bulk graciously

—to zero.

★

But the worst of speaking in the dark is that the sounds we emit are strange and hollow.

★

The moon was solemnly full.
Jim Trotmeyer assertively declared, Emotions can't be governed by rules.
Millie Corcoran politely requested, Don't overwhelm me.
To this Jim Trotmeyer delightfully responded, But the azures of spring truly rush.
Millie Corcoran remarked astutely, Azures rush, yes, but composedly.
Jim Trotmeyer mused pensively, The clouds do indeed puzzle.
Millie Corcoran said sociably, They appear above the crowd.
Oswald Proskaniewicz interrupted furiously, You, Jim Trotmeyer, are not the radical you say you are.

★

As for me, I want to be Banambitan
and leave kind ships vitalities by art.
I am untouchable.

from *Conjunctions*

The Formation of Soils

◇　◇　◇

For forty million years   a warm, warm rain—

then the sea got up to try to relax.

Vulnerable volcanoes had just melted away.

He worked below, translating the author's imps and downs,
     his ups and demons—;
pines grew skyward though the pines were not.

Thus began long episodes of quiet,

nickel laterites not ready
for the slots.

It took periods of soft showers attacking the dream
under the silt-covered sun,

Osiris washing his fragments,
Leda swimming with her vagabonds.

Everyone is made essentially the same way.

Through notebooks of tight red dirt
Franciscans walked upside down under us:

aluminum oxides,   incidents of magma,

and I had to go down in the earth for something—

Iron sediments spread over the foothills where Caliban
had his flat;

I was wearing the brown sweater when we spoke,
my heart and the one below translating his heart out.

But by that time, what.

Experience had been sent up, at an angle.

from *The Journal*

JANE HIRSHFIELD

In Praise of Coldness

◇ ◇ ◇

"If you wish to move your reader,"
Chekhov wrote, "you must write more coldly."

Herakleitos recommended, "A dry soul is best."

And so at the center of many great works
is found a preserving dispassion,
like the vanishing point of quattrocento perspective,
or the tiny packets of desiccant enclosed
in a box of new shoes or seeds.

But still the vanishing point
is not the painting,
the silica is not the blossoming plant.

Chekhov, dying, read the timetables of trains.
To what more earthly thing could he have been faithful?—
Scent of rocking distances,
smoke of blue trees out the window,
hampers of bread, pickled cabbage, boiled meat.

Scent of the knowable journey.

Neither a person entirely broken
nor one entirely whole can speak.

In sorrow, pretend to be fearless. In happiness, tremble.

from *Tin House*

113

JOHN HOLLANDER

What the Lovers in the Old Songs Thought

◇　◇　◇

Thinking "In the beginning was the—(*What??*)"
Faust tried, for openers, *Wort . . . Sinn . . . Kraft . . . Tat*
("Word"? Meaning? Power?—all these reeked of creed:
He finally settled simply on "the Deed".)
But none of these would do for true Beginning:
Our ghosts were there before all those, and not
Playing love's game in which there is no winning,
But doing love's work, continuous creation
Of all the celebrated lovers' tales,
Of all the letters, all the conversation,
All the strange fictions that plain fact entails
And all the silences that bridge the void
Of words exhausted. Let us take possession
Of Origin, then like some crafty Freud
Saying "In the beginning was Repression"
Or like some cabbalist "First was the Name."
What could we literary lovers claim?

In the beginning was unlikeness? (*Good!*)
In the beginning was the opened door
Through which crept in the soul of all our sins?　.
In the beginning there was need for more?
In the beginning there was likelihood?—
The oldest gospel of our lives begins
"In the beginning there was metaphor."

from *The New Republic*

After 65

◇ ◇ ◇

The tragedy, Colette said, is that one
does *not* age. Everyone else does, of course
(as Marcel was so shocked to discover),
and upon one's mask odd disfigurements
are imposed; but that garrulous presence
we sometimes call the self, sometimes deny

it exists at all despite its carping
monologue, is the same as when we stole
the pears, spied on mother in the bath, ran
away from home. What has altered is what
Kant called Categories: the shape of *time*
changes altogether! Days, weeks, months,

and especially years are reassigned.
Famous for her timing, a Broadway wit
told me her "method": asked to do something,
anything, she would acquiesce *next year*—
"I'll commit suicide, provided it's
next year." But after sixty-five, next year

is now. Hours? there are none, only a few
reckless postponements before *it is time* . . .
When was it you "last" saw Jimmy—last spring?
last winter? That scribbled arbiter
your calendar reveals—betrays—the date:
over a year ago. Come again? No

time like the present, endlessly deferred.
Which makes a difference: once upon a time
there was only time (. . . *as the day is long*)
between the wanting self and what it wants.
Wanting still, you have no dimension where
fulfillment or frustration can occur.

Of course you have, but you must cease waiting
upon it: simply turn around and look
back. Like Orpheus, like Mrs. Lot, you
will be petrified—astonished—to learn
memory is endless, life very long,
and you—you are immortal after all.

from *Antioch Review*

FANNY HOWE

Doubt

◇ ◇ ◇

Virginia Woolf committed suicide in 1941 when the German bombing campaign against England was at its peak and when she was reading Freud whom she had staved off until then.

Edith Stein, recently and controversially beatified by the Pope, who had successfully worked to transform an existential vocabulary into a theological one, was taken to Auschwitz in August, 1942.

One year later Simone Weil died in a hospital in England—of illness and depression—determined to know what it is to know.
She, as much as Woolf and Stein, sought salvation in a choice of words.

But multitudes succumb to the sorrow induced by an inexact vocabulary.

While a whole change in discourse is a sign of conversion, the alteration of a single word only signals a kind of doubt about the value of the surrounding words.
Poets tend to hover over words in this troubled state of mind.
What holds them poised in this position is the occasional eruption of happiness.

While we would all like to know if the individual person is a phenomenon either culturally or spiritually conceived and why everyone doesn't kill everyone else, including themselves, since they can—poets act out the problem with their words.

Why not say "heart-sick" instead of "despairing"?
Why not say "despairing" instead of "depressed"?

Is there, perhaps, a quality in each person—hidden like a laugh inside a sob—that loves even more than it loves to live?
If there is, can it be expressed in the form of the lyric line?

Dostoevsky defended his later religious belief, saying of his work "Even in Europe there have never been atheistic expressions of such power. My hosannah has gone through a great furnace of doubt."

According to certain friends, Simone Weil would have given everything she wrote to be a poet. It was an ideal but she was wary of charm and the inauthentic. She saw herself as stuck in fact with a rational prose line for her surgery on modern thought. She might be the archetypal doubter but the language of the lyric was perhaps too uncertain.

As far as we know she wrote a play and some poems and one little prose poem called *Prelude*.

Yet Weil could be called a poet, if Wittgenstein could, despite her own estimation of her writing, because of the longing for a conversion through writing her ideas down. In *Prelude* the narrator is an uprooted seeker who still hopes that a transformation will come to her from the outside. The desired teacher arrives bearing the best of everything, including delicious wine and bread, affection, tolerance, solidarity (people come and go) and authority. This is a man who even has faith and loves truth.

She is happy. Then suddenly, without any cause, he tells her it's over. She is out on the streets without direction, without memory. Indeed she is unable to remember even what he told her without his presence there to repeat it, this amnesia being the ultimate dereliction.

If memory fails, then the mind is air in a skull.
This loss of memory forces her to abandon hope for either rescue or certainty.

And now is the moment where doubt—as an active function—emerges and magnifies the world. It eliminates memory. And it turns eyesight so far outwards, the vision expands. A person feels as if she is the figure inside a mirror, looking outwards for her moves. She is a forgery.

When all the structures granted by common agreement fall away and that "reliable chain of cause and effect" that Hannah Arendt talks about—breaks—then a person's inner logic also collapses.

Yet strangely it is in this moment that doubt shows itself to be the physical double to belief; it is the quality that nourishes willpower, and the one that is the invisible engine behind every step taken.
Doubt is what allows a single gesture to have a heart.

In this prose poem Weil's narrator recovers her balance after a series of reactive revulsions to the surrounding culture by confessing to the most palpable human wish: that whoever he was, he loved her.

Hope seems to resist extermination as much as a roach does.

Hannah Arendt talks about the "abyss of nothingness that opens up before any deed that cannot be accounted for." Consciousness of this abyss is the source of belief for most converts. Weil's conviction that evil proves the existence of God is cut out of this consciousness.

Her Terrible Prayer—that she be reduced to a paralyzed nobody—desires an obedience to that moment where coming and going intersect before annihilation.

And her desire: "To be only an intermediary between the blank page and the poem" is a desire for a whole-heartedness that eliminates personality.

Virginia Woolf, a maestro of lyric resistance, was frightened by Freud's claustrophobic determinism since she had no ground of defense against it. The hideous vocabulary of mental science crushed her dazzling star-thoughts into powder and brought her latent despair into the open air.
Born into a family devoted to skepticism and experiment, she had made a superhuman effort at creating a prose-world where doubt was a mesmerizing and glorious force.

Anyone who tries, as she did, out of a systematic training in secularism, to forge a rhetoric of belief is fighting against the odds. Disappointments are everywhere waiting to catch you, and an ironic realism is always convincing.

Simone Weil's family was skeptical too, and secular while attentive to the development of the mind. Her older brother fed her early sense of inferiority with intellectual put-downs. Later, her notebooks chart a superhuman effort at conversion to a belief in affliction as a sign of God's presence.

Her prose itself is tense from sustained and solitary concentration. After all, to convert by choice (that is, without a blast of revelation or a personal disaster) requires that you shift the names for things, and force a new language out of your mind onto the page.

You have to *make* yourself believe. Is this possible? Can you turn "void" into "God" by switching the words over and over again?
Any act of self-salvation is a problem because of death which always has the last laugh, and if there has been a dramatic and continual despair hanging over childhood, then it may even be impossible.

After all, can you call "doubt" "bewilderment" and suddenly be relieved?

Not if your mind has been fatally poisoned. . . .
But even then, it seems, the dream of having *no doubt* continues, finding its way into love and work. After all choices matter exactly as much as they don't matter—especially when history is on your side.

from *Seneca Review*

Sweet Reader, Flanneled and Tulled

◇ ◇ ◇

Reader unmov'd and Reader unshaken, Reader unsedc'd
and unterrified, through the long-loud and the sweet-still
I creep toward you. Toward you, I thistle and I climb.

I crawl, Reader, servile and cervine, through this blank
season, counting—I sleep and I sleep. I sleep,
Reader, toward you, loud as a cloud and deaf, Reader, deaf

as a leaf. Reader: *Why don't you turn
pale?* and, *Why don't you tremble?* Jaded, staid
Reader, You—who can read this and not even

flinch. Bare-faced, flint-hearted, recoilless
Reader, dare you—Rare Reader, listen
and be convinced: Soon, Reader,

soon you will leave me, for an italian mistress:
for her dark hair, and her moon-lit
teeth. For her leopardi and her cavalcanti,

for her lips and clavicles; for what you want
to eat, eat, eat. Art-lover, rector, docent!
Do I smile? I, too, once had a brash artless

feeder: his eye set firm on my slackening
sky. He was true! He was thief! In the celestial sense
he provided some, some, some

(much-needed) relief. Reader much-slept with, and Reader I will die
without touching, You, Reader, You: mr. small-
weed, mr. broad-cloth, mr. long-dark-day. And the italian mis-

fortune you will heave me for, for
her dark hair and her moonlit-teeth. You will love her well in-
to three-or-four cities, and then, you will slowly

sink. Reader, I will never forgive you, but not, poor
cock-sure Reader, not, for what you think. O, Reader
Sweet! and Reader Strange! Reader Deaf and Reader

Dear, I understand youyourself may be hard-
pressed to bear this small and un-necessary burden
having only just recently gotten over the clean clean heart-

break of spring. And I, Reader, I am but the daughter
of a tinker. I am not above the use of bucktail spinners,
white grubs, minnow tails. Reader, worms

and sinkers. Thisandthese curtail me
to be brief: Reader, our sex gone
to wildweather. YesReaderYes—that feels much-much

better. (And my new Reader will come to me empty-
handed, with a countenance that roses, lavenders, and cakes.
And my new Reader will be only mildly disappointed.

My new Reader can wait, can wait, can wait.) Light-.
minded, snow-blind, nervous, Reader, Reader, troubled, Reader,
what'd ye lack? Importunate, unfortunate, Reader:

You are cold. You are sick. You are silly.
Forgive me, kind Reader, forgive me, I had not intended to step this
    quickly this far
back. Reader, we had a quiet wedding: he&I, theparson

&theclerk. Would I could, stead-fast, gracilefacile Reader! Last,
good Reader, tarry with me, jessa-mine Reader. Dar-
(jee)ling, bide! Bide, Reader, tired, and stay, stay, stray Reader,

true. *R.: I had been secretly hoping this would turn into a love poem*. Disconsolate. Illiterate. Reader,
I have cleared this space for you, for you, for you.

From *The Paris Review*

The Emperor of China

◊　◊　◊

I didn't know I was going to sleep until I woke up. . . .
—PAUL BOWLES

1

Remember the boy who played with a rope
in Kieslowski's film? He wrapped it around his hand
in the back of the taxi before he strangled the driver. Because.
Filmed through a filter, gray-green pallor of streets in a city,
moldy faces. Unnatural light the color of evil. It follows us now
when the sky is so steadily even in winter blue. Follows us
climbing the sanctified hill in Ein Kerem, the two mothers touching
each other's bellies, the unborn skimming across the valley
in their bees' wings, and a choir of children in the courtyard
of the Church of the Visitation singing Mozart.

2

Thin little squares of metal sewn in the hems of drapes
to make them hang straight. They are weighing me down.
Like the pigment and gravel in a Kiefer painting crushed
by the weight of its own excess. I don't want romance
in dung heaps, or Nuremberg with a blow-torch and traces
of blood. I don't want silence under the master's arches.
I want them to hear what I say. Disorder, chaos, the fibrillation
of my heart. I don't want us to fight the old wars.

3

"I was the eldest son of the Emperor of China. Our father
put me in a basket, summoned his mandarins in their funny caps
to rock me to sleep and fill me with nightmares about the war,
so when he died and I would be Emperor I'd be so scared
of war I'd never start one." When Uri was nine or ten in the camps
and his younger brother was frightened, he would tell him
the story again and again, how it all was a dream while he slept
in a basket and how nothing they went through was real.

4

"Enjoy your life," said our friend on her eightieth birthday,
"whether you like it or not." On the road to the *Peace
and Other Dreams Writers' Conference* in Beersheva,
a blue glass *hamsa* dangles from the rear view mirror
against the evil eye. There are fields of sunflowers
on both sides of the road. Their quivering faces follow us
down the highway, rimmed with light. They will be harvested
for oil and seeds the birds haven't stolen. I'm glad for the yellow,
that it's not at the center, that it sways and shines all the way
to the edge as long as the eye remembers.

5

The shape of a sound, your voice and the vowels as I saw them
in the first years, lips slightly open over mine and your warm
tongue bringing me here. The place of beginnings. We never
thought about the End. Where we are is only where we have been.
Diamond edge of the mind, our selves coming out of the rock
like spiked thistles. Something older than bodies that live
for a moment under the blankets, their moist skin touching.
Diamond and coal the same pure element of carbon. How you
talked about Lawrence when we first met. I want you to feel my
heart at the back of your throat. We can't go on with the quarrels
near the rubble of the next war. If we could only remember

how we started, perhaps the words would remember us
the way we found the road home in a blackout.

6

Oh love, for the young wolf caught in a foot trap in Sinai
who pulled the trap out of the ground and dragged herself
with the trap attached over our border, now healed and set free
in the desert; for the red heifers they'll never breed pure enough;
for the tiny knuckles of freesia and hyacinth breaking out of
the cold earth before it is spring; for us in our cheerfulness
and fury, for days when we're still who we were from the beginning,
unrecognized; for the Emperor of China, for dreaming and waking
though we're all dying, whether you like it or not, enjoy.

7

We're bent in the garden planting spring bulbs, pulling up
weeds, and I'm wondering how much longer we'll crouch here
on our knees in the damp soil sorting things out. Guardians
of shrubs and flowers, the first wild cyclamen sipping the sun.
We watch over each other as we watch over our garden,
woolly branches of cacti, fiery pokers of aloes in winter.
Especially during a long drought, after a snowfall, or following
the arcs of missiles on our screen. Flurries of extra caring.
Some mornings we hang on to each other as if we're afraid to let go.

8

What lasts is what we are up against. We are dividing
the city after the walls came down. Raising new barriers.
I explain why I did what I did you explain why you said
what you said and that makes it worse it gets obsessive
like our neighbor across the street who sweeps the stone path
to his front door every day and now that it's snowing
sweeps it every few hours. He's out there still in the numbing cold
wearing shorts black socks and sandals, making neat little mounds

of dirty snow. First he sweeps every pine needle out to the curb
and cleans up the sidewalk. Then he turns on the hose
and washes it down. We watch from our windows
as the soft flakes fall and he wipes them off with a rag,
wrings out the rag and wipes them again.

from *American Poetry Review*

The Quick
and the Dead

◇ ◇ ◇

At the hayfield's edge, a few stalks
of grass are twitching; I bend close
and find the plump body of the vole.
He's dead, I lobbed him here myself,
after snapping him in a mousetrap to halt
his forays through the flower beds. Yet now
he lives: he jerks, he heaves, he shudders,
as if the process of decomposition
had quickened in him and turned violent,
or he were struggling with something
blocking an attempt at resurrection—
or could it be that something
unimaginable happens, something
worse than death, after death.

I prog him, tilt him, peer under him
and see: he's being buried, by beetles—
bright-yellow or red chevrons
laid across their black wings—
carrion beetles, sexton beetles,
corpse-eating buriers who delve
and undergrub him, howking out
the trench his sausagey form settles into.

Now a beetle moils across him,
spewing at both ends, drooking him

in chemical juices. The reek of him
is heavy, swampy, surely savory,
luring from afar not only beetles
but those freeloaders of the afterlife
the midden flies, who arrive
and drop their eggs in, too,
before the covering of the grave.

Scummaging down into an ever
more formfitting last resting place,
the vole by now has dwelt almost
a full day in death, and yet somehow he's
still looking good. His gape drawn back,
he bares his teeth: uppers
stubby and old-folks yellow, lowers
an inch long, curled inward, like uppers
of beavers if forced to subsist on soft food.
At the last day, when souls go back
to their graves and resume the form
and flesh once theirs, this one
could jump and jig, as if simply
risen from a good night's dead sloom.

The flies' eggs hatch, the larvae squirm
in and out of the eyeholes; in and out
of the ears; in and out of the snout,
which slorped too often the airy auras
of our garden flowers; in and out of the mouth,
which, even cluttered with bent choppers,
snipped flowers and dragged the blossoms
stem first through gaps in the stone wall—
all but the peony blossom, which stuck
and stoppered the hole for a week
like a great gorgeous cork; and in and out
of the anus, like revenant turds,
that go in to practice going out.

The last half of the vole's tail
still sticks out, as if it might be left

that way, like a stalk of grass, to make
the site look natural. At the grave's edge
a cricket stands in glittering black,
ogling it all. Shocking to find
this hearth critter here, like a Yankee
town father spectating at a cross burning.

A larger beetle, the pronotum behind
her head brilliant red, noggles
into view; pushing the grass down
on either side she plouters
without pause past the tobacco-ish
teeth and down into the underroom
of the self-digesting birth banquet,
to deposit her eggs, to wait, and then
to peel tidbits from the carcass and feed
her hatchlings mouth to mouth, like a bird.

Soon this small plot will be unfindable:
every blade of grass will look
like a vole's tail, every smither
of ungrassed earth like burial ground,
day won't feel exactly like day, nor night
like night, and in the true night,
when we have our other, more lunatic day,
I may hear in the dunch of blood
a distant, comforting, steady shovelling,
but I will know—when a human body
is drained of its broths and filled
again with formaldehyde and salts,
or unguents and aromatic oils, and pranked
up in its holiday best and laid out
in a satin-lined airtight stainless-steel
coffin and stowed in a leakproof concrete vault—
I will know that if no fellow-creatures
can pry their way in to do the underdigging
and jiggling and earthing over and mating
and egg laying and birthing forth,
then the most that can come to pass

will be a centuries-long withering
down to a gowpen of dead dust, and not ever
the crawling of new life out of the old,
which is what we have for eternity on earth.

from *The New Yorker*

Dear Derrida

◇　◇　◇

My new grad-school roommates and I are attending
our first real lecture, which has gone okay,
we guess, since none of us understands it,
when one of our professors rises,
a somewhat prissy fellow
with a mild speech impediment,
and says he takes issue with the speaker's tone,
which he characterizes as one of "sar, sar,"
and here he raises his voice a little,
"sar, sar, sar," and wipes his mouth

with a handkerchief, "sar," and turns red
and screams, "sar, sar, sar—DAMN EET!—sarcasm!"
The four of us look at each other
as if to say, Hmmmm, nothing like this
at the cow colleges we went to!
After that, whenever we'd spill our coffee
or get a sock stuck in the vacuum cleaner,
we'd look at the mess ruefully
and say, "da, da, da—SARCASM!—damn eet!"

Our lives were pretty tightly sealed,
and if we weren't in class or the library,
either we spent our time in wordplay
or cooking: what with girlfriends
and passersby, we always had a pot
of water boiling on the back of the stove
(it's like you're ready to deliver babies,
somebody said once), either for spaghetti

or sausages, though one evening Chris,
      the English student from England, came by

for a sausage supper, and after he left,
         we ran up on the roof to pelt him
with water balloons, though when we did,
      he fell down as though he'd been shot,
and one of us said, Jeez, what's wrong
         with Chris, and somebody else said,
You know, Chris eats nothing *but* sausage,
        and a third party said, Hmmmm,
      maybe we ought to vary our diet a little.

        And that was our life: school, the boiled messes
      we made on that stove, and hanging around
that crummy apartment talking about,
        I don't know, Dr. Mueller's arm,
I guess, which hung uselessly
      by his side for reasons no one
fathomed—polio, maybe, or some
        other childhood disease—though Paul
said he thought it was made of wood.
      Can't be made of wood, said Michael,

you can see his hand at the end
        of it, to which Paul replied,
Yeah, but you can have a wooden arm
      and a real hand, can't you?
And that was what our life was like,
        because mainly we just sat around
and speculated like crazy while
      the snow piled up outside,
      so much so that by the time spring came,

        I'd had it, so I moved out of there and in with Grant
      and Brian and Poor Tom, who were philosophy
students but also genuine bad asses,
        believe it or not, because at that time
you more or less had to be an existentialist,
      i. e., tough, and not a deconstructionist,

which was a few years down the road yet
            and which would have left everyone
paralyzed, since all texts
            eventually cancel themselves out.

Of the new roomies, I hit it off best
            with Grant, who became one of the big-brother
types I seemed to be looking for at that period in my life,
            and in fact he rescued me
on more than one occasion, such as the time I was talking
            to a local girl outside a bar
called Jazz City and her three brothers
            decided to "teach me a lesson" and would have
            if Grant hadn't punched one of them

            across the hood of a parked car, or the night
he and I were in this other place where
a biker gang called Quantrill's Raiders
            hung out and into which wandered
a well-dressed couple so unaware
            of their surroundings that they asked the bartender
to please make them some hot toddies,
            which set everybody to laughing,
only the Quantrills decided we were laughing at them
            and jumped up to "teach us a lesson"

and would have, too, if Grant had not thrown
            a table at them and dragged me
out of there to dive behind some garbage cans
            and choke on our own laughter
while the drunk, fucked-up bikers howled
            and swore and punched each other since they
couldn't punch us. All this was therapy,
            I figured, since grad school was stressful enough
            to send three people I knew to the clinic

            with barbiturate overdoses (two made it,
            one didn't), and I'm not even listing here
all the divorces I know of that were directly
            attributable to that constant pressure

to be the best, be publishable, hireable,
          lovable, that came from professors and sweethearts
and parents but mainly from ourselves,
               as though each of us were two people,
a good and capable slave, on the one hand,
          and, on the other, a psychotic master

who either locked us up with our pots
               of boiling water or sent us out to dance
with the devil in the streets of Baltimore.
          That year magi appeared from the east:
Jacques Lacan, Tzvetan Todorov,
               Roland Barthes, and Jacques Derrida
brought their Saussurean strategies
               to the Hopkins conference on "The Language
of Criticism and the Sciences of Man,"

               where they told us that all language
is code and thus separate from reality,
and therefore everything
               is a text as long as there is nothing
more than this half-conscious
               linguistic interplay between perceiver
and perceived, which is another way
               of saying that language is the only reality
or at least the only one that counts.
          As different as these thinkers are,

each was telling us that there is no us:
               that cultural structures
or the media or Western thought
          or the unconscious mind
or economic systems make us
               what we are or what we seem to be, since,
in fact, we are not, which isn't such bad news,
               if you think about it, because it means
we don't have to take ourselves so seriously.

          Derrida and company make it impossible
for anyone today to read a book

as they had before, but we didn't know that then.
                Grant didn't, that's for sure;
four years later, he put a gun in his mouth
            and blew the back of his skull off,
and sometimes it makes me sad
                when I think of how long it takes
for new ideas to catch on, because,
            yeah, deconstruction might have saved us.

                from *The Kenyon Review*

The Ashes

◇ ◇ ◇

For William Gass

This elderly poet, unpublished for five decades,
Said that one day in her village a young girl
Came screaming down the road,
"The Red Guards are coming! The Red Guards . . .
Are Coming!" At once the poet
Ran into her house and stuffed the manuscript
Of her poems into the stove. The only copy.
When the guards arrived they took her into the yard
For interrogation. As they spoke
The poet's mother tried to hang herself in the kitchen.
That's all I know about the Red Guard.
It is enough.

The elderly poet is bitter—and why not?
She earned her Ph.D. at an Ivy League school
And returned to China in 1948. Bad timing.
She is bitter with me
Because I've chosen to translate a younger poet,
Young enough to be her child or mine.
The truth is, her poems are forced,
But not flowering. The good work died in the stove.
She knows this. She wants me to recompose them
From the ashes. She wants the noose
Around her mother's neck untied by me.
She wants—oh she wants!—to have her whole life over:

Not to leave America in 1948;
To know me when we are both young promising poets.
Her rusty English now is flawless,
My Mandarin, so long unused, is fluent.
No dictionaries needed. A perfect confidence
Flowing between us. And the Red Guard,
Except as the red sword-lilies
That invigilate the garden,
Unimagined by us both:
I, who believe the Reds are agrarian reformers,
She, who believes she will be an honored poet,
Her name known to everyone, safe in her fame.

from *The Texas Review*

To World War Two

◇   ◇   ◇

Early on you introduced me to young women
    in bars
You were large, and with a large hand
You presented them in different cities,
Made me in San Luis Obispo, drunk
On French seventy-fives, in Los Angeles, on
    pousse-cafés.
It was a time of general confusion
Of being a body hurled at a wall.
I didn't do much fighting. I sat, rather I stood,
    in a foxhole.
I stood while the typhoon splashed us into
    morning.
It felt unusual
Even if for a good cause
To be part of a destructive force
With my rifle in my hands
And in my head
My serial number
The entire object of my existence
To eliminate Japanese soldiers
By killing them
With a rifle or with a grenade
And then, many years after that,
I could write poetry
Fall in love
And have a daughter
And think
About these things

From a great distance
If I survived
I was "paying my debt
To society" a paid
Killer. It wasn't
Like anything I'd done
Before, on the paved
Streets of Cincinnati
Or on the ballroom floor
At Mr. Vathé's dancing class
What would Anne Marie Goldsmith
Have thought of me
If instead of asking her to dance
I had put my BAR to my shoulder
And shot her in the face
I thought about her in my foxhole—
One, in a foxhole near me, has his throat cut
    during the night
We take more precautions but it is night and it
    is you.
The typhoon continues and so do you.
"I can't be killed—because of my poetry. I have
    to live on in order to write it."
I thought—even crazier thought, or just as
    crazy—
"If I'm killed while thinking of lines, it will be
    too corny
When it's reported" (I imagined it would be
    reported!)
So I kept thinking of lines of poetry. One that
    came to me on the beach in Leyte
Was "The surf comes in like masochistic lions."
I loved this terrible line. It was keeping me
    alive. My Uncle Leo wrote to me,
"You won't believe this, but someday you may
    wish
You were footloose and twenty on Leyte
    again." I have never wanted
To be on Leyte again,
With you, whispering into my ear,

"Go on and win me! Tomorrow you may not
    be alive,
So do it today!" How could anyone ever win
    you?
How many persons would I have had to kill
Even to begin to be a part of winning you?
You were too much for me, though I
Was older than you were and in camouflage.
    But for you
Who threw everything together, and had all
    the systems
Working for you all the time, this was trivial. If
    you could use me
You'd use me, and then forget. How else
Did I think you'd behave?
I'm glad you ended. I'm glad I didn't die. Or
    lose my mind.
As machines make ice
We made dead enemy soldiers, in
Dark jungle alleys, with weapons in our hands
That produced fire and kept going straight
    through
I was carrying one,
I who had gone about for years as a child
Praying God don't let there ever be another war
Or if there is, don't let me be in it. Well, I was
    in you.
All you cared about was existing and being won.
You died of a bomb blast in Nagasaki, and
    there were parades.

from *Harper's Magazine*

NOELLE KOCOT

Consolations Before an Affair, Upper West Side

◇ ◇ ◇

The ticking minutes shed their sound.
Our ill-matched grammar claps like thunder
Over plates of noctilucent steam.
Strange, you were rich in a poor country
And now you are its mirror.
My catechism was the digital whim of this city.
I feasted on a diet of its most numinous scraps.
It seems neither one of us has obeyed
The edicts of arranged existence.
Earlier tonight I walked here with you,
Unperplexed on the perimeter of what is,
As the nimble sentences springing from your face
Revived my collection of darknesses
Strung around me like a smashed necklace of shells.
Always, this part of the city
Fills with the scent of old ghosts,
And now the tumult of new ones.
For you the undulant tomorrows seem image-laden, plaintive,
And I want to say please, be careful, but I have no right
As your hair is already stricken a little with gray.
I want to find a way to burn it into you from across the table,
Across these fine dressings of civility,
That what I have at any given moment
Is a limbo cloaking my heavy shoulders
Like a balm that soothes the phoenix.

from *Another Chicago Magazine*

Songs of the Valley

◇ ◇ ◇

There are two choirs, one poised in space,
Compelled by summer and the noise of cars
Obscured behind the green abundance of the leaves.
The other one is abstract, kept alive by words
Deflected from their courses, gathered
And assembled in the anonymity of someone's room.
Their crescendos mount like mountains of desire,
Like bodies floating through a spectral haze
Of unimagined sounds, until the masks drop,
And the face of winter gazes on the August day
That spans the gap between the unseen and the seen.
The academies of delight seem colder now,
The chancellors of a single thought
Distracted by inchoate swarms of feelings
Streaming like collegians through the hollow colonnades.
Fish swim in the rivers. Olives ripen on the trees.
And the wind comes pouring through the valley
Like the flowing monologue of the mirror,
Celebrating the rocks and hills beyond the window.
The clouds are stones set in the inner sky
Where the nights and days distill their contradictions,
The piano is the minor of a dream, and distant
Fires transmit their codes from ridge to ridge.
It is a pageant of the wistful and the real, sound
And sense, archaic figures and the eyes that see them
In absentia. Morning is a different dream,
Waking to the embarrassment of a face,
To a paradox created in the semblance of a person
Who remains a pessimist of the imagination,

Caught up in the coarse mesh of thought
Through which life flows, and is celebrated.

from *Southwest Review*

Seven Deadly Sins

◇ ◇ ◇

SLOTH

If you're one of seven
Downfalls, up in your kingdom
Of mulberry leaves, there are men
Betting you aren't worth a bullet,

That your skin won't tan into a good
Wallet. As if drugged in the womb
& limboed in a honeyed languor,
By the time you open your eyes

A thousand species have lived
& died. Born on a Sunday
Morning, with old-world algae
In your long hair, a goodness

Disguised your two-toed claws
Bright as flensing knives. In this
Upside-down haven, you're reincarnated
As a fallen angel trying to go home.

ENVY

Icarus imitated the golden plover,
Drawn toward a blue folly
Above, looping through echoes
Of a boy's prankish laughter,

Through an airy labyrinth
Of conjecture. A lifetime
Ahead of Daedalus, with noon sun
In his eyes, he outflew the bird's

Equilibrium, wondering how this
Small creature of doubt braved
The briny trade winds. Surely,
In a fanfare of uneclipsed wings

Driven by dash & breathless style,
He could outdo the plover's soars
& dares. But he couldn't stop
Counting feathers against salty sky.

PRIDE

Crowned with a feathered helmet,
Not for disguise or courtship
Dance, he looks like something
Birthed by swallowing its tail,

Woven from a selfish design
& guesswork. As if masked
With a see-through caul
From breast to hipbone,

His cold breath silvers
Panes of his hilltop house
Into a double reflection.
Silhouetted almost into a woman,

He can beg forgiveness now
As he leans against a window
Overlooking Narcissus's pond
Choked with a memory of lilies.

LUST

If only he could touch her,
Her name like an old wish
In the stopped weather of salt
On a snail. He longs to be

Words, juicy as passionfruit
On her tongue. He'd do anything,
Would dance three days & nights
To make the most terrible gods

Rise out of ashes of the yew,
To step from the naked
Fray, to be as tender
As meat imagined off

The bluegill's pearlish
Bones. He longs to be
An orange, to feel fingernails
Run a seam through him.

GLUTTONY

In a country of splendor & high
Ritual, in a fat land of zeros,
Sits a man with string & bone
For stylus, hunched over his easel,

Captured by perfection.
But also afflictions live behind
Electric fences, among hedges
& a whirlwind of roses, down

To where he sits beside a gully
Pooling desires. He squints
Till the mechanical horizon is one
Shadowplay against bruised sky,

Till the smoky perfume limps
Into undergrowth. He balls up
Another sheet in unblessed fingers, always
Ready to draw the thing that is all mouth.

AVARICE

At six, she chewed off
The seven porcelain buttons
From her sister's christening gown
& hid them in a Prince Albert can

On a sill crisscrossing the house
In the spidery crawlspace.
She'd weigh a peach in her hands
Till it rotted. At sixteen,

She gazed at her little brother's
Junebugs pinned to a sheet of cork,
Assaying their glimmer, till she
Buried them beneath a fig tree's wide,

Green skirt. Now, twenty-six,
Locked in the beauty of her bones,
She counts eight engagement rings
At least twelve times each day.

ANGER

We can cut out Nemesis's tongue
By omission or simple analysis.
Doesn't this sin have to marry
Another, like a wishbone

Worked into meat, to grow
Deadly? Snared within
The blood's quick night,
Our old gods made of sex

& wit, of nitrate & titanium,
Hurl midnight thunderbolts
& lightning. Are we here
Because they must question

Every death in an alley,
Every meltdown? We know
We wouldn't be much, if thorns
Didn't drive light into wet blooms.

from *Poetry*

Wedding Day

◇　◇　◇

1.

I have an appointment with elsewhere
I told the crater
which was filling with water and fragrant debris.
But that's just me.

All the impatient green bottles were pairing off,
a few stuffed with dainty Spanish galleons.
I doused my rag in silvery butane.
I had a picnic to attack: lamb chops; childhood.

Mine was a wedding of pipeline and pomp.
My bride pranced barefoot in the rime-dusted marsh.
She who sold me her eventual surrender
before losing herself in the blades.

She was a pristine evasive gesture.
She was a prissy evasive jester.
Troubled by a prolonged fondling
at the construction bin she called home.

2.

A confidential grimace in the ditch.
A brass band with its mouthpieces removed.

She in dejection
swung in one hand her broken heels
at the stone altar and in the other
tugged her ringlets.

The turbulent breeze had found me
and asked me to slumber in its physicist's truck.
I liked trucks. And this one's treads
had been scooped of sand with a sparkling trowel.

3.

One of the emotions not included
showed up on my fruit plate
like a seed but more like a listening
device. You've swallowed all

the mints, whispered my mate to me.
The mint with the imprint of a slave ship
and its masts and its slaves floundering at sea,
oh never to be reproduced.

Home: the chaff of stereotypical daylight,
potatoes in the closet, the waxy floor;
and squatting in shadows beneath the fuse box,
distracted by trumpets, my only lonely bride.

4.

It was solstice inside the atom
and I took a stroll
to the sandy atoll
where I hired a girl for a whirl.

There was room for me inside her and her family.
She was swollen with particles of Emerson.
She had a packet of locomotive stamps
that she longed to sell me in the future.

This is the future I said and she with longing replied:
You sir have bought yourself a shiny train.

from *Northwest Review*

The Rider

◊ ◊ ◊

Some believe the end will come in the form of a mathematical equation.
Others believe it will descend as a shining horse.
I calculate the probabilities to be even at fifty percent:
Either a thing will happen or it won't.
I open a window,
I unmake the bed,
Somehow, I am moving closer to the equation or to the horse with everything I do.
Death comes in the form of a horse covered in shining equations.
There will be no further clues, I see.
I begin to read my horse.
The equations are drawn in the shapes of horses:
Horses covered in equations.
I am tempted to hook an ankle around the world as I ride away.
For I am about to ride far beyond the low prairie of beginnings and endings.

from *American Letters & Commentary*

Tattoos

◇ ◇ ◇

1.

Chicago, 1969

Three boots from Great Lakes stumble arm-in-arm
   Past the hookers
  And winos on South State
To a tat shack. Pissed on mai tais, what harm
   Could come from the bright slate
Of flashes on the scratcher's corridor
Wall, or the swagger of esprit de corps?

Tom, the freckled Hoosier farmboy, speaks up
   And shyly points
   To a four-inch eagle
High over the Stars and Stripes at sunup.
   A stormy upheaval
Inside—a seething felt first in the groin—
Then shoves its stubby subconscious gunpoint

Into the back of his mind. The eagle's beak
   Grips a banner
  Waiting for someone's name.
Tom mumbles that he'd like the space to read
   FELIX, for his small-framed
Latino bunkmate with the quick temper.
Felix hears his name and starts to stammer—

He's standing there beside Tom—then all three
               Nervously laugh
               Outloud, and the stencil
Is taped to Tom's chest. The needle's low-key
               Buzzing fusses until,
Oozing rills of blood like a polygraph's
Lines, there's a scene that for years won't come off.

Across the room, facedown on his own cot,
               Stripped to the waist,
          Felix wants Jesus Christ
Crucified on his shoulder-blade, but not
               The heart-broken, thorn-spliced
Redeemer of punk East Harlem jailbait.
He wants light streaming from the wounds, a face

Staring right back at those who've betrayed him,
               Confident, strong,
          With a dark blue crewcut.
Twelve shading needles work around the rim
               Of a halo, bloodshot
But lustrous, whose pain is meant to prolong
His sudden resolve to fix what's been wrong.

(Six months later, a swab in Viet Nam,
               He won't have time
          To notice what's been inked
At night onto the sky's open hand—palms
               Crawling with Cong. He blinks.
Bullets slam into him. He tries to climb
A wooden cross that roses now entwine.)

And last, the bookish, acned college grad
               From Tucson, Steve,
          Who's downed an extra pint
Of cut-price rye and, misquoting Conrad
               On the fate of the mind,
Asks loudly for the whole nine yards, a "sleeve,"
An arm's-length pattern of motives that weave

And eddy around shoals of muscle or bone.
                    Back home he'd signed
          On for a Navy hitch
Because he'd never seen what he's since grown
          To need, an *ocean* which. . . .
But by now he's passed out, and left its design
To the old man, whose eyes narrow, then shine.

By dawn, he's done. By dawn, the others too
                    Have paid and gone.
          Propped on a table-top,
Steve's grappling with a hangover's thumbscrew.
          The bandages feel hot.
The old man's asleep in a chair. Steve yawns
And makes his way back, shielded by clip-ons.

In a week he'll unwrap himself. His wrist,
                    A scalloped reef,
          Could flick an undertow
Up through the tangled swash of glaucous cyst
          And tendon kelp below
A vaccination scallop's anchored seaweed,
The swelling billow his bicep could heave

For twin dolphins to ride toward his shoulder's
                    Coppery cliffs
          Until the waves, all flecked
With a glistening spume, climb the collar-
          Bone and break on his neck.
When he raises his arm, the tide's adrift
With his dreams, all his watery what-ifs,

And ebbs back down under the sheet, the past,
                    The uniform.
          His skin now seems colder.
The surface of the world, he thinks, is glass,
          And the body's older,
Beckoning life shines up at us transformed
At times, moonlit, colorfast, waterborne.

2.

Figuring out the body starts with the skin,
   Its boundary, its edgy go-between,
The scarred, outspoken witness at its trials,
   The monitor of its memories,
Pleasure's flushed archivist and death's pale herald.
   But skin is general-issue, a blank
Identity card until it's been filled in
   Or covered up, in some way disguised
To set us apart from the beasts, whose aspects
   Are given, not chosen, and the gods
Whose repertoire of change—from shower of gold
   To carpenter's son—is limited.
We need above all to distinguish ourselves
   From one another, and ornament
Is particularity, elevating
   By the latest bit of finery,
Pain, wardrobe, extravagance, or privation
   Each above the common human herd.
The panniered skirt, dicky, ruff, and powdered wig,
   Beauty mole, Mohawk, or nipple ring,
The pencilled eyebrow above Fortuny pleats,
   The homeless addict's stolen parka,
Face lift, mukluk, ponytail, fez, dirndl, ascot,
   The starlet's lucite stiletto heels,
The billboard model with his briefs at half-mast,
   The geisha's obi, the gigolo's
Espadrilles, the war widow's décolletage . . .
   Any arrangement elaborates
A desire to mask that part of the world
   One's body is. Nostalgia no more
Than anarchy laces up the second-hand
   Myths we dress our well-fingered goods in.
Better still perhaps to change the body's shape
   With rings to elongate the neck, shoes
To bind the feet, lead plates wrapped to budding breasts,
   The Sadhu's penis-weights and plasters,
The oiled, pumped-up torsos at Muscle Beach,

Or corsets cinched so tightly the ribs
Protrude like a smug, rutting pouter pigeon's.
   They serve to remind us we are not
Our own bodies but anagrams of their flesh,
   And pain not a feeling but a thought.

But best of all, so say fellow travellers
   In the fetish clan, is the tattoo,
Because not merely molded or worn awhile
   But exuded from the body's sense
Of itself, the story of its conjuring
   A means defiantly to round on
Death's insufferably endless emptiness.
   If cave men smeared their bones with ochre,
The color of blood and first symbol of life,
   Then peoples ever since—Egyptian
Priestesses, Mayan chieftains, woady Druids,
   Sythian nomads and Hebrew slaves,
Praetorian guards and kabuki actors,
   Hell's Angels, pilgrims, monks, and convicts—
Have marked themselves or been forcibly branded
   To signify that they are members
Of a group apart, usually above
   But often below the rest of us.
The instruments come effortlessly to hand:
   Fish bone, razor blade, bamboo sliver,
Thorn, glass, shell shard, nail, or electric needle.
   The canvas is pierced, the lines are drawn,
The colors suffuse a pattern of desire.
   The Eskimos pull a charcoaled string
Beneath the skin, and seadogs used to cover
   The art with gunpowder and set fire
To it. The explosion drove the colors in.
   Teddy boys might use matchtip sulfur
Or caked shoe polish mashed with spit. In Thailand
   The indigo was once a gecko.
In mall parlors here, India ink and tabs
   Of pigment cut with grain alcohol
Patch together tribal grids, vows, fantasies,

Frescos, planetary signs, pinups,
Rock idols, bar codes, all the insignia
  Of the brave face and the lonely heart.

The reasons are both remote and parallel.
  The primitive impulse was to join,
The modern to detach oneself from, the world.
  The hunter's shadowy camouflage,
The pubescent girl's fertility token,
  The warrior's lurid coat of mail,
The believer's entrée to the afterlife—
  The spiritual practicality
Of our ancestors remains a source of pride.
  Yielding to sentimentality,
Later initiates seek to dramatize
  Their jingoism, their Juliets
Or Romeos. They want to fix a moment,
  Some port of call, a hot one-night-stand,
A rush of mother-love or Satan worship.
  Superstition prompts the open eye
On the sailor's lid, the fish on his ankle.
  The biker makes a leather jacket
Of his soft beerbelly and nailbitten hands.
  The callgirl's strategic butterfly
Or calla lily attracts and focuses
  Her client's interest and credit card.
But whether encoded or flaunted, there's death
  At the bottom of every tattoo.
The mark of Cain, the stigma to protect him
  From the enemy he'd created,
Must have been a skull. Once incorporated,
  Its spell is broken, its mortal grip
Loosened or laughed at or fearlessly faced down.
  A Donald Duck with drooping forelock
And swastikas for eyes, the sci-fi dragon,
  The amazon's griffon, the mazy
Yin-yang dragnets, the spiders on barbed-wire webs,
  The talismanic fangs and jesters,
Ankhs and salamanders, scorpions and dice

All are meant to soothe the savage breast
Or back beneath whose dyed flesh there beats something
That will stop. Better never to be
Naked again than not disguise what time will
Press like a flower in its notebook,
Will score and splotch, rot, erode, and finish off.
Ugly heads are raised against our end.
If others are unnerved, why not death itself?
If unique, then why not immortal?
Protected by totem animals that perch
Or coil in strategic locations—
A lizard just behind the ear, a tiger's
Fangs seeming to rip open the chest,
An eagle spreading its wings across the back—
The body at once both draws death down
And threatens its dominion. The pain endured
To thwart the greater pain is nothing
Next to the notion of nothingness.
Is that what I see in the mirror?
The vacancy of everything behind me,
The eye that now takes so little in,
The unmarked skin, the soul without privileges . . .
Everything's exposed to no purpose.
The tears leave no trace of their grief on my face.
My gifts are never packaged, never
Teasingly postponed by the need to undo
The puzzled perfections of surface.
All over I am open to whatever
You may make of me, and death soon will,
Its unmarked grave the shape of things to come,
The page there was no time to write on.

3.

New Zealand, 1890

Because he was the chieftain's eldest son
And so himself
Destined one day to rule,

The great meeting-house was garishly strung
        With smoked heads and armfuls
Of flax, the kiwi cloak, the lithograph
Of Queen Victoria, seated and stiff,

Oil lamps, the greenstone clubs and treasure box
        Carved with demons
        In polished attitudes
That held the tribal feathers and ear drops.
        Kettles of fern root, stewed
Dog, mulberry, crayfish and yam were hung
To wait over the fire's spluttering tongues.

The boy was led in. It was the last day
        Of his ordeal.
        The tenderest sections—
Under his eyes, inside his ears—remained
        To be cut, the maze run
To its dizzying ends, a waterwheel
Lapping his flesh the better to reveal

Its false-face of unchanging hostility.
        A feeding tube
        Was put between his lips.
His arms and legs were held down forcibly.
        Resin and lichen, mixed
With pigeon fat and burnt to soot, was scooped
Into mussel shells. The women withdrew.

By then the boy had slowly turned his head,
        Whether to watch
        Them leave or keep his eye
On the stooped, grayhaired cutter who was led
        In amidst the men's cries
Of ceremonial anger at each
Of the night's cloudless hours on its path

Through the boy's life. The cutter knelt beside
        The boy and stroked
        The new scars, the smooth skin.

From his set of whalebone chisels he tied
          The shortest one with thin
Leather thongs to a wooden handle soaked
In rancid oil. Only his trembling throat

Betrayed the boy. The cutter smiled and took
          A small mallet,
          Laid the chisel along
The cheekbone, and tapped so a sharpness struck
          The skin like a bygone
Memory of other pain, other threats.
Someone dabbed at the blood. Someone else led

A growling chant about their ancestors.
          Beside the eye's
          Spongy marshland a frond
Sprouted, a jagged gash to which occurs
          A symmetrical form,
While another chisel pecks in the dye,
A blue the deep furrow intensifies.

The boy's eyes are fluttering now, rolling
          Back in his head.
          The cutter stops only
To loop the blade into a spiralling,
          Puckered, thick filigree
Whose swollen tracery, it seems, has led
The boy beyond the living and the dead.

He can feel the nine Nothings drift past him
          In the dark: Night,
          The Great Night, the Choking
Night, the All-Brightening Night and the Dim,
          The Long Night, the Floating
Night, the Empty Night, and with the first light
A surging called the War Canoe of Night—

Which carries Sky Father and Earth Mother,
          Their six sons borne
          Inside the airless black

———
162

The two make, clasped only to each other.
        Turning onto his back,
The eldest son struggles with all his force,
Shoulder to sky, straining until it's torn

Violently away from the bleeding earth.
            He sets four beams,
        Named for the winds, to keep
His parents apart. They're weeping, the curve
        Of loneliness complete
Between them now. The old father's tears gleam
Like stars, then fall as aimlessly as dreams

To earth, which waits for them all to return.
            Here is the care
        Of the dead, and his tears
Seep into her folds like a dye that burns.
        One last huge drop appears
Hanging over the boy's head. Wincing, scared,
He's put his hand up into the cold air.

from *The Paris Review*

Mae West Chats It Up
with Bessie Smith

◇　◇　◇

You hadn't oughta kiss a girl if you're carrying a gun.
—RAYMOND CHANDLER

once I found a cowboy   who thought he could
ride me into the New   West and God
put rollers on the bed   to make his journey smoother
last time I saw him   he looked the worse for wear
hair all but gone   gut eating his belt
he was a sight   all laid out in a new suit
(same one I bought him)

honey he had a corvette   and the morals
of a chinchilla   but just enough
gangster to satisfy my   Kansas City longings
oh he was handsome   as you know the devil was
in his eyes and his clothes   slick as sharkskin
some kinda silk worn close   and groin sweet
like morning rain   inside a buttercup

cept he dropped his pants and showed me
something for the cat to play with

thought he'd stopped me on the road
he did but when I said come up and see me
I was already heading in another direction

then there was that business   with some woman
he wouldn't name   now would naming matter sugah
you gotta know who you're aiming for   just aim
for the light   of one cigarette to the next
always someone there with a match   and an itch
to scratch   what hurts long as your voice holds

from *Crab Orchard Review*

My One

◇ ◇ ◇

and only: money

minus one. No noun
like a pronoun!—best of all

the jealous kind. Come, come,
company doll, cide with a coin,

one moan, one
more, honey

bunch.

from *Jubilat*

Music for Homemade Instruments

◊ ◊ ◊

improvising with Douglas Ewart

I dug you artless, I dug you out. Did you re-do? You dug me less, art. You dug, let's do art. You dug me, less art. Did you re-do? If I left art out, you dug. My artless dug-out. You dug, let art out. Did you re-do, dug-out canoe? Easy as a porkpie piper-led cinch. Easy as a baby bounce. Hop on pot, tin pan man. Original abstract, did you re-do it? Betting on shy cargo, strutting dimpled low-cal strumpets employ a hipster to blow up the native formica. Then divide efficiency on hair-nets, flukes, faux saxons. You dug me out, didn't you? Did you re-do? Ever curtained to experiment with strumpet strutting. Now curtains to milk laboratory. Desecrated flukes & panics displayed by mute politi-cians all over this whirly-gig. Hey, you dug! Art lasts. Did you re-do? Well-known mocker of lurching unused brains, tribal & lustrous did-dlysquats, Latin dimension crepe paper & muscular stacks. Curtains for perky strumpets strutting with mites in the twilight of their origami funkier purses. Artless, you dug. Did you re-do? For patting wood at flatland, thanks. For bamboozle flukes at Bama, my seedy medication. Thanks for my name in the yoohoo. Continental camp-out, percolat-ing throughout the whirly-gig on faux saxon flukes. You dug art, didn't you? Did you re-do?

from *Facture*

Our Kitty

◇　◇　◇

She is swinging in a contraption above the heads
of the audience,
　　　　Reflected in the glass lamps on the tables.

She sits in one of those fin-de-siècle gilded sleighs
hung from the ceiling
　　　　by braids of sparkling hemp.

Here come all the poet-accountants pushing in
to talk about cate-
　　　　gories of experience. Wine, sex.

The ceiling is hammered tin, alight and jumping
with her shadow
　　　　cast upward by the table lamps.

As she swings, she rubs herself, adjusts herself
in the seat, so she
　　　　can be seen through the see-through bottom.

Pink cheeks has Kitty. A pop-open camisole. Mother
is striking her
　　　　name from the family bible. But

she has to eat, does Kitty. She is so petite and incautious
that all the poet-
　　　　accountants are taking copious notes.

They can use her: she may be the littlest
Whore of the imagination.
                She might even be how they imagine

The twentieth century's end: just like the end
of the last century,
                the dream of body parts floating

Above cigar smoke. In other words, *more war.*
Kitty inspires all
                of them to think about triage.

The end of the twentieth century. Artist or banker—
who should be saved?
                The artist in his same old tourniquet? The banker

With a dented skull? Try to guess. The poet-
accountants have
                already guessed. They know the price of

this ending. They've seen the banker and his surgeons,
the poet bleeding
                all over the sterile gauze. Who wants to be

John Keats? Well, the poems, yes—but not the death.
Now they hear Kitty
                coughing. I'm Keats, she gasps.

I'm John Fucking Keats returned in Kitty's body.
Forlorn she cries *Forlorn*
                but they refuse to listen to her

As she swings, pale and beautiful, glittering above them
holding out her
                living hand, warm, capable—as ever, untaken.

from *The Evansville Review*

ALICE NOTLEY

Where Leftover Misery Goes

◇   ◇   ◇

if its a spiritual offense does it as wrongdoing take place more in more in the second

leftover

or spiritual world and is the significance of the double now that i might be might the one who offends in other circumstan or that it takes two to make an offense but how was i used and why were the others not usable was it because they were always too selfinvolved to be exploited. oh keep this mostly masked as always these events are of the sort are replayed over and over in the second world perhaps in the overlap the border was it a spiritual offense and did it take place more in the second world than in the first it surely does now. it only takes place in my and keep this masked keep it low shes awaiting attention acceptance as exceptional her face corroding i have to avoid her like poison but i have to keep remembering shes poison there is a machine that allows memory to be memories to taken into the futur i have to remember shes pois and that isnt a known a universally accepted fact that shes poison to me wants to poison me and make me hers of her emotional her emotional camp make me live of the camp of she thinks but she is poison shes acting like she isnt and i can barely remember the last time i was poisoned and now in the now in the second world there is no linear time no many years past and i dont know when they last said in the first world accept her poison bu because its only you dont bother us on the cold wintry avenue in your coat lined with papers another wild looking night darker than the last one which was purple this ones deep navy with sliver moon behind a raggy cloud in this wind the buildings are dangerously high and here and there a gold lights tossed i didnt see the two strangers my former fr is that possible strangers until i suddenly did

staring at me but the real point is that i'm not them nor her i'm not the double and i
want to be hard about this i am only the double as i must straddle two worlds but i am
th not the double who did wrong to me i am not thee there is no key for the brilliant
red lake in the top of the rectangle map of me which seems to be a sort of early area is
desperation a pleasure i'm so thirsty and i'm suppose in joy but do i believe remem
desperation joy or guilt approach me from a side street trying to make me talk to them
i'm singing a song and the he double says not enough facts in that song though theres
a lot of poetry one word has become coeur of me what word it must be poet coeur de
coeur no longer no longer a word we have driven up high to this mountain town
where the gypsies live but must leave live but must leave he asks me to talk to him
but i wont now an she all fuzzed up in the head wants to give me an entire shelf of
old books as a bribe to poison knowledge of her mind but i'm resolutely in black fur
burning into a snowbank a dream a tall snowbank that is taller than i am and its hard
to walk hard to walk here in the death you are helping i am being assimilated and
wear a long dress and shawl watch me make love as a prostitute so i can be your friend
because youve only ever wanted to see my body what you think of me the villagers
want to circumcize me sunday so i can be everyones theyre gypsies in the mountains
on luna something street i used to live there but i have since cut up the sidewalk and
carry it with me carry luna something street with me wherever i go and lay it down so
i can walk towards or away what away from what i must walk away from them again
board the ship my other sister life will go to the camp where the actress a second a
second

demonic womans face must be kept out of the movie you cant know about her you cant know in the first world and in the second thus there are these dreams which play out shadows on the street useless kindness curiously useless until the play the playing out is over in the head of what you did used me to stay you and so i'm a gypsy again wait for the camp to break up in the mountains encased in crystal you used me but said you were use in the first world on the street on the street of poison words b was it only words no there was the deathhole that was burned into the snow it was supposedly another who died not die because i was never the one was i never the focus was other so how could you ever affect me when you were trying to ki fight another and only poison me lightly who died not die but there was the deathhole burned into the snow here in the second world as i play it out play it out in the crystal a lighter story now where i never die have only died to that world. no one believes in poison thats why we cant breathe. someone has left me a book highlighted in black always do that leave a book and the letters hop and try to transform but tha they cant nor can the shelf of old book of esoterica change the nature of poison which goes towards because only because only thinks of self thinks story so the poison flows outwards in the bad air in winter tinged with yellow and corroded face bookstore bookstore ever if the double lives in a book. others support her because i have never needed story and the letters hop and try to transform they are snow the letters try again i dont know how to tell you this letters i dont care about your transitional stages i dont care why you used pois i dont care whose real name or person i dont have to be tain tained certain of the action of self without salt keep doing this keep doing this so old. because it happened once in the first world and in the second doesnt quite go away the actions in the first and the real story as dream as dream in the seconds milder haunt where who died not i but died to the first and died to that camp and died to that bookstore and died to that oh keep this mostly masked dont feel a thing or be pois get poisoned theyre still all waiting for that i dreamed i lived them they wore black robes and lived in a cluster of wooden houses in a clearing but there may have been woods and i was being assimilated i wore a long black dress and shawl the narrator cut in to say that i was prostitute and my boyfriend john watched me make love with the village men there seem to be many and tenderfaced what does prostitution symbolize half of the villagers are leaving and then i will be circumcized because he dies or somethi take part in the rite of becoming a woman can withstand of pain of that she tries to poison again wants me to be on a side and not in i wake up for a few minutes fall back asleep many years ago they are gypsies this movie will star us and the stars are familiar in the part where i'm taken away on a ship with other prisoners but am no one just movie stars just parts and theres no point in falling in love with the commandant hes just a star and i'll die anyway theres no point in and when she says love theres no love. this is a spell to get out of here how long will it take the border is endless. wants me to be on another side she wants t wants me to be on her side of the border and i stay on the side of the second world always but am still in the border the border where the nightmare sucks me into its feeling want to say her keep saying

saying

about her because no has believed it and so say it and say and so remain in the border

will the circumcized women feel after death will the real w will the real e include
sensation that cant be manipulated by ones feel fellowcreatures on the street denying
me to the point of point because i think they like and if you maintain sides you are
always near the border and never in the snows come again and the purple sinister sky
so i can die and read the books they leave me always alive the letters and the letters letters
hop about and try to change but never do because no one wants them to change.

from *Chain*

SHARON OLDS

His Costume

◇　◇　◇

Somehow I never stopped to notice
that my father liked to dress as a woman.
He had his sign language about women
talking too much, and being stupid,
but whenever there was a costume party
he would dress like us, the tennis balls
for breasts—balls for breasts—the long
blond wig, the lipstick, he would sway
his body with moves of gracefulness
as if one being could be the whole
universe, its ends curving back to come
up from behind it. Six feet, and maybe
one-eighty, one-ninety, he had the shapely
legs of a male Grable—in a short
skirt, he leaned against a bookcase pillar
nursing his fifth drink, gazing
around from inside his mascara purdah
with those salty eyes. The woman from next door
had a tail and ears, she was covered in Reynolds Wrap,
she was Kitty Foyle, and my mother was in
a tiny tuxedo, but he always won
the prize. Those nights, he had a look of daring,
a look of triumph, of having stolen
back. And as far as I knew, he never threw
up, as a woman, or passed out, or made
those signals of scorn with his hands, just leaned,
voluptuous, at ease, deeply
present, as if sensing his full potential, crossing

over into himself, and back,
over, and back.

from *The New Yorker*

The Nature of Things

◇   ◇   ◇

(after paintings by Robert Lostutter)

For ages and ages, they couldn't have seemed less simpatico—street songs turned Brahms' insane cadenza turned sharpening crack.

Which reminded you of all the novels you might have inhabited, of your daddy the routeman, of Easter's spice-flavored jelly eggs, of the rowdy oleander, of the women at the xerox place, so petty. How privately (you simmered) Time can walk, or fall.

Heart. Couldn't. Break. That was the problem here. A lonely boy. You were, just.

There must be no self-pity, your pal said then. *And that means NO self-pity. Can we not do this anymore, please?* Emanation of a wood fire, blue of blue, singleton, scamp: We live not only in a world of thoughts, but also in a world of things.

He did you a favor, your pal, when he told you this secret: *First become ordinary, if you ever wish to become anything else.* By Tuesday, you were so splendid the bees rose.

from *Barrow Street*

GRACE PALEY

Here

◇   ◇   ◇

Here I am in the garden laughing
an old woman with heavy breasts
and a nicely mapped face

how did this happen
well that's who I wanted to be

at last   a woman
in the old style   sitting
stout thighs apart under
a big skirt   grandchild sliding
on   off my lap   a pleasant
summer perspiration

that's my old man across the yard
he's talking to the meter reader
he's telling him the world's sad story
how electricity is oil or uranium
and so forth   I tell my grandson
run over to your grandpa   ask him
to sit beside me for a minute   I
am suddenly exhausted by my desire
to kiss his sweet explaining lips

from *The Massachusetts Review* and *Poetry Daily*

Untitled (February 2000)

◇   ◇   ◇

The naked woman at the window
her back to you, bowing the violin

behind the lace curtain
directly above the street

is not a fiction
as the partita is not a fiction

its theme and variations
ornaments and fills

not a fiction
as the one-way street still

wet from all this
rain is no fiction

and nakedness not a fiction.
It reads us like a book

as we listen to its music
through milky eyes wide shut.

And what does this fiction think of us?
The rain, the notes, both softly fall.

Slight errors of intonation do not matter
in the faded green

notebooks where we record these
things, and conceal other things.

What's the name of that tree, anyway,
with yellow flowers, small silver leaves,

planted in the concrete—
I used to know.

As for today, Leap Year Day,
the window was empty.

from *Conjunctions*

JOHN PECK

A Metal Denser Than,
and Liquid

◇　◇　◇

What sets the worst architect apart from the best bee is this:
the architect builds his structure in imagination before he
erects it in reality.

　　　　　　　　　　　　　　　　—MARX, *CAPITAL*

　　　Had he sat there, a witness?
at Posen, the speech in which Himmler
spoke the abomination,
a darkness within darkness.

He tried to believe he had not.
There was enough in him
that he had to go on living.
And so he would not remember.

There had been talk, briefly,
of his being made successor.
Before the complexities.
He didn't talk about that.

　　　Then there was the hospital,
when he had nearly died
from the task and the unspoken.
No one did that task better.

Doing it better became
his way of foxing the wolves

who pranced around him. But
how much had he taken on

else, and where had it led him?
He worked from that bed till he broke.
Then lift-off, out of his body:
light, rich appointments, warm colors,

the doctors did a ballet,
and at last, there at last
he felt for his wife how much,
he smiled the withheld, he fully

was who he knew he was
and knew he could go. But was sent back.

His prison chaplain, although
supposing the story might be
fantasy, knew it came with
the urgent stink of Lazarus.

Ach it was all in his mind
laughed Frau Speer. If only
she too could have seen it:
he'd nearly found the exit

from his squeeze, he'd skirted
the suck of the great change.

      And one of my own tribe: when
transferred for interrogation
to Versailles, what saved him
was an English parachute major
taking him for a drive
to Paris.
            We went through
St. Germain and Bougival
where in years past I dined
with Vlaminck, Alfred Cortot—
then we walked along the quais

182

and looked at the stalls. I was
horribly sad, but I bought
a print like any tourist
and—so silly—it made
me feel human.

   And if I briefly abhor
this fantast while pitying him
the hole in his feeling, with
art as surrogate—if
his uncontrollable falseness
even to himself, the untracked
changeability,
alarms and disgusts me?
                              Then
somewhere near right here
I have lost the treasure
of shaming accuracy
about myself.
                  His decades
of fox-introspection
kindle several days
of fascination and
gnawing discomfort and
discernment in my corner,

while a voice both sharp and soothing
intervenes: *discernment*
is not judgment!
                  May it
be so. But this rankling rawness?

Cicero did not warn us:
Aesop makes tricky reading.

Art is not surrogate,
but the gate. The gate stands
to be passed through. The passage
is to truth truly lived

whatever the means, however
mean, for what is great
and shines quiveringly is
self-presence from the soul.

　　Where the treasure lies
there lie the means also.
The metallurgist's kit
went with the gold galleons
to the bottom. Divers brush
scum from lakes of it there,
push at it, play with it,
quivering mercury—

a comeliness past that
of gold, because it lives,
a mirror to the will
to undergo all change.

Unloved, the master in him
went seeking a mad attachment.

Suddenly undersea,
the day, the room, strangely
rich in appointments, when evil
seems to shake far beyond me.

Mirror, mirror, on the floor,
which beast in me shall I adore

judiciously?
　　　　　May his rootless soul
have felt, somewhere, compassion.
Let compassion rise
and quiver in me. And let me
turn again to the sun.

from *AGNI*

LUCIA PERILLO

The Ghost Shirt

◊　◊　◊

—Museum of Natural History, NYC, 5/1/92,
the first day of the riots

The blue whale swam through blue air in the basement
while upstairs the elephants twined together tusk by tusk,
and the enormous canoe was being rowed by the Tlingit

as they have rowed without moving for years through the dusk
in the Hall of the Americas. Empty space
was brocaded by schoolkids' shrieks

as teachers pantomimed in front of each glass case,
and I turned a corner and came up smack against the ghost shirt,
worn by a mannequin with no legs and no face—

                                        at first
it almost didn't register;
it was not what books had led me to expect: no beads
no ornament no chamois leather

or those shiny cornets made from rolled up snuff-tin lids.
Instead it was just a cotton shift
negotiating grimly between blue and green and red,

with some glyphs scrawled amateurishly across the breast
in ordinary pen: a thunderbird and some lightning,
a buffalo and its hoofprint,

one tree, one little man puffing
on a flume-sized pipe. Pentagram stars formed a cloud
atopside a smaller species of stippling

that I had to stare at a long time before I understood
meant bullets. Then I found myself checking for broken threads
to see if any of the holes were rimmed in blood—

but no: time or moths or bullets, it was anybody's guess.
A quote on the wall from the Paiute messiah
said *Indians who don't believe in the ghost dance*

will grow little, just about a foot high,
and stay that way. Then some of those
will be turned into wood and burned in fire—

and I left the museum wondering about which was worse:
to display a man's blood here
so every kid can practice crumpling as if falling off a horse

(& the kid knows exactly how to clutch the new air
entering his heart). Or to clean the shirt
as if the ghost blood had never been there.

                    ★★★

This is the kind of story you could carry around
like a beaded key chain from a tourist trap:
how the ghost dance became a thunderstorm
that even summoning Buffalo Bill out
to the Standing Rock agency could not slake—
until the schoolhouses were empty
and the trading stores were empty
and the winter wheat went bony in the field
and the War Department had no idea what it meant
but that the Sioux had gone mad with their dancing
and that Yellow Bird wore a peculiar shirt when he chanted
Your bullets will not go toward us right before they did.

★★★

From the museum, I take the subway downtown
and change trains where the tunnels all converge
below Times Square, in one dank cavern underground

whose darkness seems so large it does not have edges.
Even at midafternoon, the shade there seethes
with people marching in a lockstep through that passage;

sometimes, when directed back over a shoulder, a mouth
on someone's profiled face will drop
and I'll see the tongue dart nervously along the teeth . . .

then the march becomes a gallop
when the walls begin to pound with an arriving train,
its riders rushing toward us in a yellowness crushed up

against the glass. And we board like cattle, one person
driving an elbow into another's gut
as we jam in (and we jam in . . .)

and coming up at Grand Central, I find it likewise knotted
with people ranged in single files,
shuffling toward the ticket counters in fits and stops

that give them time to paw the vast floor with their heels.
But what strikes me most is how loudly the silence
murmurs off the marble tiles

as if we were all underwater, hearing backward our own breath.
Then I remember that I bought a return on my way in
and hurry back down two flights of steps

to the lower level, where the train for Croton
sits almost full, though not scheduled to leave for half an hour
yet. Soon all the seats are gone

but the train keeps filling, arms and legs the mortar
in a wall of breasts and double-breasts. I avoid the gaze
and glare of those who hang on straps over

my head, and it isn't until the train begins to wheeze
from its hydraulics and slowly labors
past the gate that everyone around me will unfreeze

enough to speak: about a city bus and its passengers
rocked onto its flank and set aflame, a hundred black
and Spanish kids aswarm with Molotovs and crowbars . . .

which is the story we sow along the darkness, until the track
rises into daylight above Ninety-seventh Street,
where the broken windows have been boarded back

with plywood, each painted with its own domestic scene
—curtains gathered primly or potted geraniums on the sills—
though otherwise, everything looks to me as it has always been,

with the same nimbuses of spray paint on the trestles,
the alphabet stuffed like heavy furniture
reciting its addition on the same brick walls

. . . until we cross the East River
where everybody lets their breath go with relief,
the wheels droning their steady whuckerwhuckerwhucker

as the train settles into its top speed
and we skitter along the Hudson, where nothing is except
water on one side, on the other side a ravine

overstudded with junk: a Cadillac sunk axle-
deep a shopping cart the front wheels of a stroller
menacingly airborne like the forelegs of *Tyrannosaurus rex*—

and it's here the train zippers
to an abrupt stop (though we haven't come to any station),
steeping us anxiously awhile in quiet, until the whispers

blossom like umbrellas opening before the rain:
first *they're blocking the engine* then *they're lying down
on the tracks,* rumors that ripple through the train

like a wave sweeping upstream, then back down,
by which time the muttering has escalated to a shout
that goes *Keep going!* and *We've got to run those fuckers down!*

★★★

Between the train and whoever lies down in its path,
you could say there's a ghost shirt,
whatever it is that makes the locomotive stop
if the engineer can see far enough ahead.
I think it is a dotted line
looping the outskirts of our being human—
ghostly because of the ease with which
its perforations can be ripped. Also
because the sole proof of its presence
lies in the number of days we go unhurt,
a staggering number, especially when you consider
how much bigger the world is than a train.
And how something even as small as a bullet
can pick out of elsewhere's 359 degrees
one shape, and suddenly everything is changed,
though the calx of what didn't happen
remains in curiously enduring traces
like the stone casts that larval caddis flies
leave behind them in the stream
(& *larvae:* from the latin word for ghost).
What you have is always less
a history of a people, any people,
than a history of its rocks: first a heap
then a cathedral and soon a heap again,
while the names get amortized like money.
Like Damian Williams, the one they called Football,
who held his bloody cinderblock aloft
and danced as if he were stomping out a hundred

baby flames: Rodney King, Reginald Denny,
William Cody, Stacey Koon. And Black Coyote,
who refused to give up his Winchester
after Yellow Bird danced the first few steps
before Colonel Forsythe's pony soldiers
broke all hell loose. And Black Coyote,
whom Turning Hawk said was crazy,
"a young man of bad influence and in fact a nobody."

★★★

I want to say that we weren't all white on that train,
but mostly we were—
and when without explanation the engine started up again,

those who weren't fell away to the edge of the herd
and got off where the conductor squawked out *Spuyten Duyvil*,
Marblehead and *Yonkers* . . .

and as we rolled I strained to imagine the sound a wheel
would make as it milled through someone's ribs,
listening for them bedded down in every mile

until I got off way out in the suburbs.
From the station I called my father to come pick me up
and waited for him half-hidden in some shrubs

so that when he arrived I could make my usual leap
into his Mercedes so no one sees me getting in.
I remember what it was like in that town, growing up

so out of it I didn't even see the affluence back then—
and how we kids rolled our eyes whenever our parents
started in on the WPA and the Great Depression

and being glad for a day's honest work even if that meant
no more than laying a stone and piling another on top
—part of a war we waged in serial installments,

mostly over what we put on our backs, or feet, or not:
the tattered clothes we wore to ape a poverty
about which our folks claimed we did not know shit

(though like every kid in that town I toted around my copy
of a gospel that one week was *Soul on Ice*
and the next week *Bury My Heart at Wounded Knee*)

—which maybe explains why it still makes me nervous,
though twenty years have passed: to be riding around in a car
that cost more than, elsewhere, someone's house,

while I'm trying to explain to my old father
what it meant to me to see the ghost shirt
just before Wall Street shut down and every broker

fled. And not just fled, but reverted,
as if what made us human had been only a temporary crust
on our skins, as if there were no way to stop the backward

march into the swamp. Pretty soon we'd all be just
like rats but bigger, and combat ready . . .
but here again my father claimed I didn't know whereof

I spoke: all day the television had showed the city
eerily at peace. And the only fires were the tiny flames
of people holding candles, outside the public library.

from *Pequod*

The Clearing

◇ ◇ ◇

Had the light
changed, possibly—or,

differently, was that how I'd
seen it

      always, and not
looking? Was I meant for

a vessel? Did I only
believe so and,

so, for a time, was it true but

only in that space which belief makes
for its own wanting?

*What am I going to
do with you*
      —Who just

said that?

Whose the body—where—that voice
belongs to?

      Might I turn,
toward it, whinny

into it?

My life
a water,

or a cure for
that which no water
can cure?

His chest
a forest, or a lush
failure—

Even now, shall I choose? Do I
get to?

Dearest-once-to-me

Dearest-still-to-me

Have I chosen
already,

or is choice a thing
hovering yet, an

intention therefore, from
which, though
late, could I hurry back?

What am I going to do with you—   or

how?
Whom for?

If stay my hand—where

rest it?

from *Callaloo*

ROBERT PINSKY

Jersey Rain

◇ ◇ ◇

Now near the end of the middle stretch of road
What have I learned? Some earthly wiles. An art.
That often I cannot tell good fortune from bad,
That once had seemed so easy to tell apart.

The source of art and woe aslant in wind
Dissolves or nourishes everything it touches.
What roadbank gullies and ruts it doesn't mend
It carves the deeper, boiling tawny in ditches.

It spends itself regardless into the ocean.
It stains and scours and makes things dark or bright:
Sweat of the moon, a shroud of benediction,
The chilly liquefaction of day to night,

The Jersey rain, my rain, soaks all as one:
It smites Metuchen, Rahway, Saddle River,
Fair Haven, Newark, Little Silver, Bayonne.
I feel it churning even in fair weather

To craze distinction, dry the same as wet.
In ripples of heat the August drought still feeds
Vapors in the sky that swell to drench my state—
The Jersey rain, my rain, in streams and beads

Of indissoluble grudge and aspiration:
Original milk, replenisher of grief,
Descending destroyer, arrowed source of passion,
Silver and black, executioner, font of life.

from *The Atlantic Monthly*

A short narrative of breasts and wombs in service of Plot entitled

◊   ◊   ◊

Liv lying on the floor looking at

The Dirty Thought

[The womb similar to fruit that goes uneaten will grow gray fur, the breasts a dying rose, darkening nipples, prickling sickness as it moves toward mold, a spongy moss as metaphor for illness.]

Liv, answer me this: Is the female anatomically in need of a child as a life preserver, a hand, a hand up? And now, and now do you want harder the family you fear in fear of all those answers?

Could you put fear there as having to do with the price of milk, as having to do with prudence? To your health. Cheers. Or against the aging body unused, which way does punishment go?

"Let us not negotiate out of fear . . ." butbutbut . . . Then the wind touched the opened subject until Liv finding herself in light winds, squalls, was without a place to put her ladder.

From the treetop something fell, a bundle, a newspaper, a bug, a bag, still nobody's baby. The sound was desperation dropped down, a falling into place, and not way away—

Statistics show: One in what? One in every what? A child in every pot will help the body grow? No matter, all the minutes will still slip into the first then the ashes will shiver.

Liv, is the graffitied mind sprained? Who sprayed an answer there? Which cancer? What dirtied up intention? No matter. Anyway, which way does your ladder go?

Toward? Or away in keeping with that ant crawling on your ankle? Oh mindless hand, rub hard. Not quite in pain because pain is shorthand for what? One in every what? Cradle all.

Or kiss it up without facing yourself. Knowing the issue, Liv slouches, her chin resting on her folded hands. She thinks: blunt impact, injury. She tosses a but against the wall,

she tosses: boom. boom.

from *Verse*

Architect

◇ ◇ ◇

Nothing he had done before
        or would try for later
                will explain or atone
this facile suggestion of cross-beams
languid elevations traced on water
his stake in white colonnades cramping his talent
                        showing up in
facsimile mansions overbearing the neighborhood
his leaving the steel rods out of the plinths
    (bronze raptors gazing from the boxwood)
You could say he spread himself too thin   a plasterer's term
        you could say he was then
skating thin ice   his stake in white colonnades against the thinness of

ice itself   a slickened ground
        Could say he did not then love
his art enough to love anything more
Could say he wanted the commission so
badly betrayed those who hired him   an artist
        who in dreams followed
            the crowds who followed him

Imagine commandeering those oversize those prized
        hardwood columns to be hoisted and hung
by hands expert and steady on powerful machines

    his knowledge using theirs as the one kind does the other
                    (as it did in Egypt)

—while devising the little fountain to run all night
outside the master bedroom

from *The Paris Review*

Vectors: Forty-five Aphorisms and Ten-second Essays

◇　◇　◇

1.

It's so much easier to get further from home than nearer that all men become travelers.

2.

Of all the ways to avoid living perfect discipline is the most admired.

3.

Idolaters of the great need to believe that what they love cannot fail them, adorers of camp, kitsch, trash that they cannot fail what they love.

4.

Say nothing as if it were news.

5.

Who breaks the thread, the one who pulls, the one who holds on?

6.

Despair says *I cannot lift that weight.* Happiness says, *I do not have to.*

7.

What you give to a thief is stolen.

8.

Impatience is not wanting to understand that you don't understand.

9.

Greater than the temptations of beauty are those of method.

10.

Harder to laugh at the comedy if it's about you, harder to cry at the tragedy if it isn't.

11.

Patience is not very different from courage. It just takes longer.

12.

Even at the movies, we laugh together, we weep alone.

13.

I could explain, but then you would understand my explanation, not what I said.

14.

If the saints are perfect and unwavering we are excused from trying to imitate them. Also if they are not.

15.

Easy to criticize yourself, harder to agree with the criticism.

16.

Tragic hero, madman, addict, fatal lover. We exalt those who cannot escape their dreams because we cannot stay inside our own.

17.

Every life is allocated one hundred seconds of true genius. They might be enough, if we could just be sure which ones they were.

18.

Absence makes the heart grow fonder: then it is only distance that separates us.

19.

How much less difficult life is when you do not want anything from people. And yet you owe it to them to want something.

20.

Where I touch you lightly enough, there I am also touched.

21.

If we were really sure we were one of a kind, there would be no envy. My envy demeans both of us—no wonder it is the hardest sin to confess. It says I am not who I think I am unless I have what you have. It says that you are what you have, and I could have it.

22.

Laziness is the sin most willingly confessed to, since it implies talents greater than have yet appeared.

23.

If you reason far enough you will come to unreasonable conclusions.

24.

The one who hates you perfectly loves you.

25.

What you fear to believe, your children will believe.

26.

Of our first few years we remember nothing: experience only slowly gives us the power to be formed by experience. If this were not true, our characters would be completely determined by our infant hours of darkness, pain and helplessness, and we would all be the same. For her first six months my daughter cried continuously, who knows why. Yet she is as happy and trusting and kind as if all that had never happened. It never did.

27.

The road not taken is the part of you not taking the road.

28.

We invent a great Loss to convince ourselves we have a beginning. But loss is a current: the coolness of one side of a wet finger held up, the faint hiss in your ears at midnight, water sliding over the dam at the back of your mind, memory unremembering itself.

29.

If I didn't spend so much time writing, I'd know a lot more. But I wouldn't know anything.

30.

The wounds you do not want to heal are you.

31:

When my friend does something stupid, he is just my friend doing something stupid. When I do something stupid, I have deeply betrayed myself.

32.

If I didn't have so much work to keep me from it, how would I know what I wanted to do?

33.

My deepest regrets, if I am honest, are not things I wish were otherwise, but things I wish I wish were otherwise.

34.

I lie so I do not have to trust you to believe.

35.

Opacity gives way. Transparency is the mystery.

36.

To me, the great divide is between the talkative and the quiet. Do they just say everything that's on their minds, even *before* it's on their minds? Sometimes I think I could just turn up my head like a Walkman so what's going on there could be heard by others. But there would still be a difference. For inside the head they are talking to people like them, and I am talking to someone like me: he is quiet and doesn't much like being talked at; he can't conceal how easily he gets bored.

37.

Anger has been ready to be angry.

38.

It's easier to agree on the future than the past.

39.

Only half of writing is saying what you mean. The other half is preventing people from reading what they expected you to mean.

40.

They gave me most who took most gladly of my love.

41.

Back then I wanted to be right about my estimate of my abilities. Now I want to be wrong.

42.

Time heals. By taking even more.

43.

Self-love, strange name. Since it feels neither like loving someone, nor like being loved.

44.

What I hope for is more hope.

45.

To feel an end is to discover that there had been a beginning. A parenthesis closes that we hadn't realized was open).

from *Ploughshares*

What We Heard About the Japanese

◇　◇　◇

We heard they would jump from buildings
at the slightest provocation: a low mark

On an exam, a lovers' spat
or an excess of shame.

We heard they were incited by shame,
not guilt. That they

Loved all things American.
Mistrusted anything foreign.

We heard their men liked to buy
schoolgirls' underwear

And their women
did not experience menopause or other

Western hysterias. We heard
they still preferred to breastfeed,

Carry handkerchiefs, ride bicycles
and dress their young like Victorian

Pupils. We heard that theirs
was a feminine culture. We heard

That theirs was an example of extreme
patriarchy. That rape

Didn't exist on these islands. We heard
their marriages were arranged, that

They didn't believe in love. We heard
they were experts in this art above all others.

That frequent earthquakes inspired insecurity
and lack of faith. That they had no sense of irony.

We heard even faith was an American invention.
We heard they were just like us under the skin.

What the Japanese
Perhaps Heard

Perhaps they heard we don't understand them
very well. Perhaps this made them

Pleased. Perhaps they heard we shoot
Japanese students who ring the wrong

Bell at Hallowe'en. That we shoot
at the slightest provocation: a low mark

On an exam, a lovers' spat, an excess
of guilt. Perhaps they wondered

If it was guilt we felt at the sight of that student
bleeding out among our lawn flamingos,

Or something recognizable to them,
something like grief. Perhaps

They heard that our culture
has its roots in desperate immigration

And lone men. Perhaps they observed
our skill at raising serial killers,

That we value good teeth above
good minds and have no festivals

To remember the dead. Perhaps they heard
that our grey lakes are deep enough to swallow cities,

That our landscape is vast wheat and loneliness.
Perhaps they ask themselves if, when grief

Wraps its wet arms around Montana, we would not prefer
the community of archipelagos

Upon which persimmons are harvested
and black fingers of rock uncurl their digits

In the mist. Perhaps their abacus echoes
the shape that grief takes,

One island
bleeding into the next,

And for us grief is an endless cornfield,
silken and ripe with poison.

from *Verse*

Furtherness

◇   ◇   ◇

An oak coffin covered with vines
carried on moss in a farm cart

A dusty coffin in a yellow wagon
with bright red wheels going down
the painted road

A glass coffin stifled by roses

Raining, and in the film version
an unknown god stood at a distance
watching, got in his car and left

The little black urn before
a spray of orchids in the alcove

They laid a bunch of violets at her throat
closed the white coffin
carried it out the rear door
through buttercups down to the grave

The musicians are drunk and play
loudly, stumbling down the street

Six men with sore arms

The family in a rowboat:
the coffin inhabiting the mind

Or ashes streaming like a scarf from the convertible

Or, the chorus breaks out in excelsis

Or, the soloist sang like a dilated eye

Stunning din of a sob

Salt pork on a wound

Is it ordure to speak of the widow's grief?

Who drags herself back
through a field so thick with vetch
it gives a purple tint over two or three acres
You could run through them for hours
but one thing is certain from her face
she does not want you to

Furthermore, there are pies on the table waiting

from *American Letters & Commentary*

Along Overgrown Paths

◇　◇　◇

The road crowds houses almost into the lake.
On one side one day they may go plop
a short drop down a bluff a mere bank.
On the other side houses cling to it
(the road) for dear life, passing in cars
one might roll right in, well, at
the door. A first arrival by lunar eclipse:
it won't ever lose an aura of mystery
of a moon eroding and changing to the orange
of bloodroot sap. One of those roasting hot
Easters. Trilliums popped out of the ground
and unfurled at your feet before your eyes.
It was that hot. "I want," the man said,
"my stairs twice as wide as other stairs."
That was one day in 1823. They still are.
Not so high as some, wider than most,
beds can go up and down in ease and do.
Far better a hall than that extra room.
Far better a dining room than a nook.
Or a nook than a cranny or a cranny
than nothing, unless enclosed as in
this roadside hall, with wide stairs
to descend and walk out onto violets
blue, blue-violet, white, and brickish-pink
and the private houses could touch
if they'd a mind to put out their hands.

from *The New Yorker*

Night Picnic

◊   ◊   ◊

There was the sky, starless and vast—
Home of every one of our dark thoughts—
Its door open to more darkness.
And you, like a late door-to-door salesman,
With only your own beating heart
In the palm of your outstretched hand.

All things are imbued with God's being—
She said in hushed tones
As if his ghost might overhear us—
The dark woods around us,
Our faces which we cannot see,
Even this bread we are eating.

You were mulling over the particulars
Of your cosmic insignificance
Between slow sips of red wine.
In the ensuing quiet, you could hear
Her small, sharp teeth chewing the crust—
And then finally, she moistened her lips.

from *Boston Review*

Apple

◇ ◇ ◇

If I could come back from the dead, I would come back
for an apple, and just for the first bite, the first
break, and the cold sweet grain
against the roof of the mouth, as plain
and clear as water.

Some apple names are almost forgotten
and the apples themselves are gone. The smokehouse,
winesap and York imperial, the striped
summer rambo and the winter banana, the little
Rome with its squat rotunda and the pound apple

that pulled the boughs to the ground.
The sheep's nose with its three-pointed snout,
the blue Pearmain, speckled and sugared.
Grime's golden, cortland, and stamen.
If an apple's called "delicious," it's not.

Water has no substance
and soil has no shell,
sun is all process
and rain cannot rise.
The apple's core carries

a birth and a poison.
Stem and skin, and flesh,
and seed, the apple's name,
no matter, is work
and the work of death.

If you wait for the apple, you wait
for one ripe moment. And should
you sleep, or should you dream, or
should you stare too hard in the daylight
or come into the dark to see

what can't be seen, you will drop
from the edge, going over into
coarse, or rot, or damping off.
You will wake to yourself, regretful,
in a grove of papery leaves.

You need a hillside, a small and steady wind,
a killing frost, and, later, honey-bees.
You need a shovel, and shears, and a ladder

and the balance to come back down again.
You will have fears of codling moths
and railroad worms, and aphids.

Scale and maggots and beetles
will come to do their undoing.
Forests will trap the air

and valleys will bend to gales—
cedars will bring on rust, so keep them
far in the distance. Paradise,

of course, was easy, but you and I live
in this world, and "the fruit of the tree
in the midst of the garden"

says nothing specific about apples;
the "apples of gold" in Proverbs
are probably oranges instead.

And so are the fruits
Milanion threw down:
an apple does not glitter.

If you're interested in immortality
it's best to plant a tree, and even
then you can't be sure that form

will last under weather.
The tree can break apart in a storm
or be torqued into pieces over many

years from the weight of its ruddy labor.
The state won't let you burn the wood
in the open air; the smoke is too dense

for breathing. But apple-wood
makes a lovely fire, with excellent
heat and aroma.

Fire will take in whatever it can
and heat will draw back
into earth. "Here is the fruit,
your reward and penalty
at once," said the god

to the waiting figures.
Unbearable, the world
that broke into time.
Unbearable, the just-born
certainty of distance.

You can roast late apples
in the ashes. You can run
them in slices on a stick.
You can turn the stem to
find the letter of your love

or chase them down with
your chin in a tub.
If you count the seeds to tell
the future, your heart will
sense more than your

tongue can say. A body
has a season, though
it may not know it
and damage will bloom
in beauty's seed.

If I could come back from the dead, I would—
I'd come back for an apple,
and just for one bite, one break,
and the cold sweet grain on the tongue.
There is so little difference between

an apple and a kiss, between desire
and the taste of desire.
Anyone who tells you other-
wise is a liar, as bad
as a snake in the quiet grass.

You can watch out for the snake and the lie.
But the grass, the green green wave
of it, there below the shadows of the black
and twisted boughs, will not be
what you thought it would be.

from *TriQuarterly*

Meteor

◇   ◇   ◇

I chose this. To be this
stone, grow nothing. I wanted this
absolute position in the heavens
more than anything, than you,
my two, too beautiful, my children.
A man I knew once
muttered in his terrors of the night,
no, no, no, instead of yelling.
It was this, this dismal low,
that made me leave him. I will leave them.
All the butterflies the lord above
can muster, all their roses.
I will leave whatever colors
struggle to be noticed. To leave,
to leave. That's the verb I am,
have always been, always will be,
heading, like a dewdrop, into steamy
confrontation, my train of neutral green
lasting half a second
before casting off its freight—his arms
outside the sheet, how warm they were,
like Rome the year it burned,
Nero at the window, loving no one,
fusion crust. I fly because
my space is crossed

with fear and hair and tail and hate,
the bowels of a lioness,
iron in her roar.

from *The Journal*

The Diagnosis

◇ ◇ ◇

Lincoln was sixty years old when the doctor told him he only had forty more years to live. He didn't tell his wife, with whom he confided everything, or any of his friends, because this new revelation made him feel all alone in a way he had never experienced before. He and Rachel had been inseparable for as long as he could remember and he thought that if she knew the prognosis she would begin to feel alone, too. But Rachel could see the change in him and within a couple of days she figured out what it meant. "You're dying," she said, "aren't you?" "Yes, I'm dying," Lincoln said, "I only have forty years." "I feel you drifting away from me already," she said. "It's the drifting that kills you," Lincoln whispered.

from *LIT*

I stopped writing poetry . . .

◇　◇　◇

*Poetry gives no adequate return in money, is expensive to
print by reason of the waste of space occasioned by its form,
and nearly always promulgates illusory concepts of life.*
—MYLES NA GCOPALEEN (FLANN O'BRIEN)

No one is more confident than a bad poet.
—MARTIAL

I stopped writing poetry
When I was just starting to get good at it. First
I got good at rhyme, so I cast it away.
Then I got good at line and stanza construction—
So good I hardly needed to *say* anything at all.
My meanings emerged
                        in the spaces between.
So I got rid of that, too. Metaphor, metonymy,
Allusive echoes of my betters—well, frankly,
I was a whiz at that stuff pretty early on.
So I emptied out the file-drawers
Of rhetorical strategy, musical form,
Continuity or criticism of tradition,
And I just wrote. Finally I found
I was writing . . . *prose,* like everyone else.
But it was prose with a difference: prose with a rich,
Totally hidden other life lying behind it, unglimpsed
(I think) by the reader. Not like a prostitute
Who reforms and becomes a nun. I've seen
That movie. More like a nun who becomes a prostitute.

I stopped writing poetry
at 16 (seriously), then again at about 20
but only for six months, once again
at 27, then at 32, 35, 40, and 42.
I'll keep you posted.

i stopped writing poetry
when i realized that i understood romantic and symbolist
poetry sound sculpture objective verse conceptual art
pure language the confessional and elegiac modes and still
everything i wanted to do in poetry pretty much everything
i wanted anyone at all to do had been done already and much
better by don marquis in the archy and mehitabel poems

I stopped writing poetry
when everyone else did—in the early 90s, when television
became more interesting than culture.

I stopped writing poetry
when they came and deactivated my poetry button

I stopped writing poetry
when I got married—I mean settled down—
since the laws of the state of Maryland do not allow me
to marry the love of my life—though I'm not here
to whine about it—and maybe marriage would ruin me
as it seems to have ruined others—but one thing I know—
it is certainly nice to have someone to blame
for taking it easy and resisting inspiration when it inconveniently
insists on arising occasionally no matter what you do
(PS thanks for the dashes Emily Dickinson)

I stopped writing poetry
because the last thing I ever wanted
was to develop some obnoxious false
self masquerading as *voice* the way artists
as soon as their style becomes identifiable
are stuck in it and in what it will allow them
to think style isn't a correlative of personality
or a way to explore transcendent issues

that lie beyond mere worldly content style is
exhaustion ennui and fashion and death

I stopped writing poetry
when I received the praise of people I admired.
It's a terrible thing to receive exactly the attention you want
when you are unprepared to admit you might deserve it.
Of the many ways in which poets are always going on
about how poetry not only receives inspiration from love
but imitates it in form and feeling, this just may be the worst.

I stopped writing poetry because I saw what it was doing to people's prose style.
        Yikes.

I stopped writing poetry—
well, basically, because I'm white. I don't
like being white, it isn't a choice I'd make freely,
and to get argumentative I don't think it's entirely fair
that I have to be white right now when it's so 10 minutes ago
when if I'd been born fifteen years earlier most racists
would have considered me anything but, what with
the whole Jew-as-vermin thing, but OK, OK, I concede
the point, I'm culturally white, or whatever, *dammit,*
and in case you haven't noticed, this just isn't
white people's moment, poetry-wise. Don't even
get me *started* on the griot tradition and that stuff,
I mean, just look at rap—poetry that communicates
exquisitely within its chosen boundaries of class
and common interest, and hardly at all outside it,
except for those to whom it stands as aspiration to cool.
Just like Shakespeare and Donne. What have white people
contributed to culture recently? *Postmodernism?* Please.
My own revelation came when I realized
Little Red Corvette meant more to me than any poem
published since the early 1970s. On the not-very
mean streets where I learned versification, poetry
wasn't a mode of expression spontaneously developed
from living people's lived experience, it was a *regime.*
Well, that's over now. Get over it.

I stopped writing poetry
When I just ran out of steam.
It's really not a whole lot
More complicated than that.

I stopped writing poetry
When my friends started dying. Some of my friends
Wrote beautifully about the conditions of their illness,
And insightfully about mortality and their own impending
Death. Some wrote angrily about their invisibility
And created a literature of testimony in which we learn
What it was like to walk in the streets of American cities
As a ghost. Some wrote poems to memorialize their lovers,
Or to embarrass right-wing senators or arts funding agencies.
But I just counted 67 people I knew and was fond of
Who've died of "AIDS-related illness," and not once
Have I genuinely felt I could respond to their suffering or death
In poetry. Is it poetry? Is it me? The era? I am willing to believe
That if Milton and Shelley and Tennyson could do it,
It can still mean something. Why should I think their ages
Made death any more manageable a subject than mine?
But whenever I sat down to try, I stopped in despair.
Whatever the political advantages of slogans
Of the time, it wasn't the right words I looked for
But some way to make silence heard in lines
Of verse, and I never found it.
                                        Now even that
Sounds like a device to me, like special pleading.
Fuck it. Just fuck it. Let someone else do it.

I stopped writing poetry
but I still love the stanza. All that other cool stuff—
tropes, the caesura, enjambment—I can live without.
But the *stanza*—wow.

I stopped writing poetry
after I went to my first MLA conference,
where they were attacking a way of reading
and understanding literature they called
"mainstream" and "dominant" that I'd never even

encountered. It was like what they meant by "book"
was totally different from what I meant by "book"—
as different as "washing machine" and "golf ball."
I stopped writing poetry when it was eclipsed by criticism
for purely sociological and economic reasons.
I stopped writing poetry when people began writing
scholarly articles explaining how to read Frank O'Hara's
Lunch Poems and it never occurred to them to mention
that you should read them during lunch. I stopped
writing poetry when it became popular. I realize
Robert Frost read at Kennedy's inauguration but now
Ethan Hawke is telling *Vanity Fair* that he keeps
your book by his bed, and poetry as adjunct
to commercial culture and the veneration of celebrity
is so much more deliciously embarrassing for everyone
than even poetry in the service of the state.
I stopped writing poetry when taking it seriously
started seeming more likely to indicate
intellectual complacency than intellectual liveliness.
I stopped writing poetry when it got boring.

I stopped writing poetry
when the internet replaced the telephone
(since now that *everyone* has a phone,
and takes it *everywhere*, it's obvious
the telephone is *over*). Ted Berrigan I thought
destroyed the sonnet by inviting the beloved
to just pick up the phone and call him
sometime—thus no more need to plead
and seduce through verse—so the *channel*
changed: it works both ways. Now we are all
(gay str8 bi-curious) pleading and seducing
in lower case as only the freest verse used to
hitting reply b4 the intimacy of communication
has time even to register killing off poetry
by creating the first real audience for it in centuries

I stopped writing poetry
because I promised to. I read something
at the Ear Inn around 1984 in which I encouraged everyone

to give up writing—as I engaged to—and it went over
real big. Afterwards any time I ran into any of the
poetry crowd they'd always ask me if I was still
not writing. I understood it was a performance piece
and so did they but I kept getting this gnawing feeling
I was abandoning a principle by continuing to write.
It was entirely superstition, like actually feeling sick
when you call in sick, but I suppose I have been a victim
of the terrible conviction that you must mean what you say.

I stopped writing poetry
when I had dedicated poems to everyone I knew, at least everyone I wanted to
        impress.
I promise to start writing poetry again as soon as I meet some new people.
Interesting people, anyway.
Interesting people I can't just come out and *say* things to, anyway.

I stopped writing poetry
but as satisfying as it has been to turn my back on it
as on a distant homeland fallen under the spell of a fascist party
still a breeze reaches me from time to time fragrant of verse
and suddenly I am as nostalgic as an exiled Russian
grand duke waiting on tables in Paris in a screwball comedy
sometimes I wonder would it really be so terrible
if I wrote just one more line

from *Antioch Review*

DEAN YOUNG

Sources of the Delaware

◊   ◊   ◊

I love you he said but saying it took twenty years
so it was like listening to mountains grow.
I love you she says fifty times into a balloon
then releases the balloon into a room
whose volume she calculated to fit
the breath it would take to read
the complete works of Charlotte Brontë aloud.
Someone else pours green dust into the entryway
and puts rice paper on the floor. The door
is painted black. On the clothesline
shirt-tails snap above the berserk daffodils.
Hoagland says you've got to plunge the sword
into the charging bull. You've got
to sew yourself into a suit of light.
For the vacuum tube, it's easy,
just heat the metal to incandescence
and all that dark energy becomes a radiance.
A kind of hatching, syntactic and full of buzz.
No counter-indications, no laws forbidding
buying gin on Sundays. No if you're pregnant,
if you're operating heavy machinery because
who isn't towing the scuttled tonnage
of some self? Sometimes just rubbing
her feet is enough. Just putting out
a new cake of soap. Sure, the contents
are under pressure and everyone knows
that last step was never intended to bear
any weight but isn't that why we're standing there?
Ripples in her hair, I love you she hollers

over the propellers. Yellow scarf in mist.
When I planted all those daffodils,
I didn't know I was planting them
in my own chest. Play irretrievably
with the lid closed, Satie wrote on the score.
But Hoagland says he's sick of opening
the door each morning not on diamonds
but piles of coal, and he's sick of being
responsible for the eons of pressure needed
and the sea is sick of being responsible
for the rain, and the river is sick of the sea.
So the people who need the river
to float waste to New Jersey
throw in anti-depressants. So the river
is still sick but nervous now too,
its legs keep thrashing out involuntarily,
flooding going concerns, keeping the president
awake. So the people throw in beta-blockers
to make it sleep which it does, sort of,
dreaming it's a snake again but this time
with fifty heads belching ammonia
which is nothing like the dreams it once had
of children splashing in the blue of its eyes.
So the president gets on the airways
with positive vectors and vows
to give every child a computer
but all this time, behind the podium,
his penis is shouting, Put me in, Coach,
I can be the river! So I love you, say
the flashbulbs but then the captions
say something else. I love you, says
the hammer to the nail. I love Tamescha,
someone sprays across the For Sale sign.
So I tell Hoagland it's a fucked-up ruined
world in such palatial detail, he's stuck
for hours on the phone. Look at those crows,
they think they're in on the joke and
they don't love a thing. They think
they have to be that black to keep
all their radiance inside. I love you,

the man says as his mother dies
so now nothing ties him to the earth,
not fistfuls of dirt, not the silly songs
he remembers singing as a child.
I love you, I say meaning lend me twenty bucks.

from *Volt*

RACHEL ZUCKER

*In Your Version of Heaven
I Am Younger*

◇   ◇   ◇

In your version of heaven I am blond, thinner,
but not so witty. In the movie version of your version
of heaven you fight God to come back to me.
It is a box office hit because you are an unbelievable character.
Nothing is real except the well-timed traffic accident
which costs 226 thousand dollars.

In real life, I am on a small bridge over a small creek.
Then it isn't a bridge but a stadium. Then a low table.
A sense of knowing the future.
There is no clear location of fear.
I want you to say you will abandon your dissertation.
I want you to ask the man in the green scrubs if I was pregnant.

Put on the preservers! they announce. *They are under your seats!*
Time to tell your wife a few last things. People are puking
in the rows around us. The jackets sweaty and too big.
We are, in this version, an image of hope.
The broadcasters are just now sniffing us out.
I am pregnant but don't know it and can't know
that the fetus would have been, in any event, not viable.
No one survives. No one comes down with cancer.
The fade-out leaves a black screen over the sound of water.

The review says it is a *film noir.* The letter to the editor
says the reviewer should go back to college. The reviewer

is in graduate school writing a thesis about movies
that were never made. If they are made he will not get tenure.
If we die he has a small chance at success. A young woman
writes in: *it should, more properly, have been called an embryo.*

You say I have a dark vision. You buy me coffee and muffins
and cross the street safely. In this version you are there
when I come home. Night after night in bed
beside me. By day I watch the world your eyes watch:
the blondes, the redheads, the light blue baby jogger.
In this version the camera has a tiny light leak and the film,
after reediting, has no blond and no plane and no preservers.
No metaphysical struggle, no hero, no chance for financial success.

from *American Poetry Review*

CONTRIBUTORS' NOTES AND COMMENTS

NIN ANDREWS was born in Charlottesville, Virginia, in 1958. She has published three books of poetry: *The Book of Orgasms* (a new expanded version of which is just out from Cleveland State University), *Spontaneous Breasts* (Pearl Editions, 1998), which won the Pearl Chapbook Contest, and *Why They Grow Wings* (Silverfish Press, 2001), winner of the Gerald Cable Prize of 2000. She lives in Poland, Ohio.

Of "Notes for a Sermon on the Mount," she writes: "A couple of years ago I was at a Buddhist retreat where the teacher lectured on the sacredness of the body, which she said was the same as the holiness of Mother Earth. 'We need to start respecting every aspect of our physical selves,' she said. She led us on a guided meditation in which we were supposed to feel gratitude for our every body part and 'to imagine it as an aspect of God, herself.' The woman sitting next to me had a lot of trouble with the exercise. She told me afterwards that she got stuck on the genitals and never made it to any other part of her body. She kept thinking of pornographic magazines and feeling slimy. The more she tried to think nice thoughts, the more uncomfortable her thoughts became. 'I just can't imagine the pussy as a part of God,' she complained. When I giggled, she told me I should write a poem with the title 'How the Pussy Is Like a God.' I had no intention of doing so. Then one day, weeks later, I was seated at this coffee shop in Poland, Ohio, trying to write my Buddhist friends when someone turned the radio on. A zealous Christian preacher was broadcasting over the airwaves. The preacher kept bellyaching about God and our Satanic New Age. Even Christianity, he said, is becoming demonized by the worship of crystals and angels. 'Thou shalt put no other gods before thee,' he kept announcing in his heavy southern accent, and I decided I needed him in the poem. I made a few changes of course, beginning with 'Thou shalt put no other pussies before thee.' And 'Thou shalt not take the name of the pussy in vain.' This poem includes the notes from that summer afternoon."

RAE ARMANTROUT has published seven books of poetry, including *Made To Seem* (Sun & Moon, 1995), *writing the plot about sets* (Chax, 1998), *Necromance* (Sun & Moon, 1991), *Couverture* (Les Cahiers de Royaumont, 1991). Her prose memoir, *True,* was published by Atelos in 1998. A new collection of poetry, *The Pretext,* is forthcoming from Green Integer. Wesleyan University Press will publish her selected poems, *Veil,* in 2001. *A Wild Salience: The Writing of Rae Armantrout,* featuring essays by Robert Creeley, Hank Lazer, Bob Perelman, Charles Alexander, Ron Silliman, Brenda Hillman, Fanny Howe, and others has recently appeared from Burning Press. Armantrout has taught writing courses at UC San Diego since the early 80s. This year she is writer in residence at the California College of Arts and Crafts. She lives in San Diego.

Armantrout writes: " 'The Plan,' like many of my poems, is written in three quasi-independent sections. Each section is separate in that each has a different context, literally refers to a different situation. What interests me is the way such separate parts can interpenetrate (affect/inflect) one another. The first section is a take on the Garden of Eden story. The second might be located in a hotel where a pair of kinky lovers meet. I'm interested in seeing what sparks fly when such scenarios bump into each other."

JOHN ASHBERY was born in Rochester, New York, in 1927. *Some Trees,* his first book, was selected by W. H. Auden for the Yale Younger Poets Prize of 1956. Ashbery lived in Paris for ten years. During part of that time he was art critic for the *International Herald Tribune.* He won the Pulitzer Prize, the National Book Award, and the National Book Critics Circle award in poetry for *Self-Portrait in a Convex Mirror* (1975). He is the Charles P. Stevenson, Jr., Professor of Language and Literature at Bard College. *Other Traditions* (Harvard University Press, 2000) consists of the Norton lectures he gave at Harvard on such poets as John Clare, Thomas Lovell Beddoes, Raymond Roussel, David Schubert, and Laura Riding. *Your Name Here* (Farrar, Straus and Giroux, 2000) is his latest book of poems. In 2001 he was named state poet of New York. He divides his time between Hudson, New York, and New York City. He was guest editor of *The Best American Poetry 1988.*

ANGELA BALL was born in Athens, Ohio, in 1952. She cites her good luck in having, pro forma, to attend college right there, at Ohio University, where Victor Depta suggested to her that her tiny works were more ur-poems than ur-stories, and Stanley Plumly taught her the ineffables that make a poem. She later earned an M.F.A. from the University of Iowa and a Ph.D. from the University of Denver. She now teaches in the Center for Writers at the University of Southern Mississippi, where she is an editor for *Mississippi Review* (her World Poetry issue appeared in spring 2000). In spring 1999, she was poet in residence at the University of Richmond. She has received grants from the Mississippi Arts Commission and the National Endowment for the Arts. Her books include *Kneeling Between Parked Cars* (Owl Creek Press, 1990); *Possession* (Red Hen Press, 1995); *Quartet,* consisting of four long poems in the voices of Sylvia Beach, Nora Joyce, Nancy Cunard, and Jean Rhys (Carnegie Mellon University Press, 1995); and *The Museum of the Revolution,* a collage poem on Cuba (Carnegie Mellon University Press, 1999). "Jazz" is part of a recently completed manuscript, *Sleepy Girl.*

Ball writes: "I think I'd call 'Jazz' a mood poem. I find I'm interested more and more in a poetry of passing moods because I believe (with Wallace Stevens) that that's where we live. It's also a tribute to mixing: imitation, theft, borrowing—generally running away with the music. I love running away with a little Charles Mingus—his brilliant elegy for Lester Young, 'Goodbye Pork Pie Hat.' And a little of the Blues, part of my long-adopted Mississippi. Also, I've realized lately that the appearance of food in my life as compared to my work has been very disproportionate, and (between meals) I want to correct that."

MARY JO BANG was born in Waynesville, Missouri, in 1946, and grew up in St. Louis. She earned a B.A. and M.A. in sociology from Northwestern University; a B.A. in photography from Westminster University (London), and an M.F.A. in poetry from Columbia University. She has published three books of poems. *Apology for Want* (University Press of New England, 1997) was awarded the Bakeless Prize and the Great Lakes Colleges Association New Writers Award; *Louise in Love* (Grove, 2001) received an Alice Fay di Castagnola Award from the Poetry Society of America; and *The Downstream Extremity of the Isle of Swans* (University of Georgia Press, 2001) won the University of Georgia Press Contemporary Poetry Series Competition. She has been a poetry editor at *Boston Review* since 1995. In 1999–2000, she was a Hodder Fellow at Princeton University. She currently teaches at Washington University in St. Louis.

Of "Crossed-Over, Fiend-Snitched, X-ed Out," Bang writes: "Like many of my poems, this one is an amalgamation of a number of seemingly unrelated events—here, the televised aftermath of the fatal plane crash of John F. Kennedy Jr. and his wife, Carolyn Bessette Kennedy, and her sister, Lauren Bessette, which occurred in July 1999; a visit to the Freud Exhibit at the Jewish Museum in New York City; a listing in a catalogue of the Freud Museum which reads, '99C. (O) Napkin ring with the portrait of the newly married couple'; and a comment by the Chinese painter, He Gong, that the tail of a small plane seen through a window in his painting, *The Un-Biblio Story*, represents the beginning of the Twentieth Century (the first flight by the Wright Brothers was in 1903). Freud and the Kennedys and aviation coalesce as a way of talking about a century's ending which, in turn, becomes a way of talking about many different kinds of endings, public and private. About the way the fevered hopes of early life invariably give way to death, and death to eventual erasure. But tonally the poem chooses ironic detachment over lament. Freud would undoubtedly have much to say about such a choice."

CAL BEDIENT was born in Grand Coulee, Washington, in 1935. He did graduate work at Cornell University and the University of Washington and went on to become a professor of English at UCLA. He has published one book of poetry, *Candy Necklace* (Wesleyan, 1997), and four books of criticism: *Architects of the Self: George Eliot, D. H. Lawrence, and E. M. Forster* (University of California Press, 1972); *Eight Contemporary Poets* (Oxford University Press, 1974); *In the Heart's Last Kingdom: Robert Penn Warren's Major Poetry* (Harvard University Press, 1984); and *He Do the Police in Different Voices: The Waste Land and its Protagonist* (University of Chicago Press, 1986). *Eight Contemporary Poets* was nominated for a National Book Award. Bedient is an editor of the New California Poetry Series (University of California Press).

Bedient writes: "I thought I saw the phrase 'when the gods put on meter' while browsing in the Upanishads (S. Radhakrishnan's edition for Indus/HarperCollins), but haven't since been able to find it. Death lay like unbreathable smoke over the antique cabin camp in the Cascades that summer: Earl and Jeanne Smith, the owners, died as summer began, a short time apart, suddenly, senselessly. (A cancellation sign seemed to run through the camp itself, a rustic survival from the 1920s that the Smith family had built by hand from local cedar where two wild rivers meet.) The individual life is a sacrifice to what? What not on earth could merit the pains of a life, or, to turn it around, the tribute of formal beauty, formal behavior, exalted language? Is the universe as a great Fate beauty or horror?

"Looking back on the poem, I think it moves to get to the place in such questioning that Adorno thought the very essence of art, namely a prehistoric shudder. At least it doesn't want to rest short of that—that in which there is no rest."

ELIZABETH BISHOP (1911–79) was born in Worcester, Massachusetts, grew up in New England and Nova Scotia, and was educated at Vassar College. She lived for long periods in Key West, Florida, and in Brazil. She won the Pulitzer Prize for *A Cold Winter* (1955), the National Book Award for *Questions of Travel* (1965), and the National Book Critics Circle Award for *Geography III* (1976). *The Complete Poems, 1927–1979* was published by Farrar, Straus and Giroux in 1983. A year later the same publisher brought out her *Collected Prose*.

Like the majority of Bishop's poems, "Vague Poem" was published first in *The New Yorker*. It is among the fifty or sixty unfinished poems found in her papers at the Vassar College library, and it will appear in a volume of posthumous works that Farrar, Straus and Giroux will publish under the title *Edgar Allan Poem and the Jukebox*. As her friend Lloyd Schwartz has observed, in her lifetime Bishop published very few poems with an explicitly sexual content. Since her death, however, many of the poems that have surfaced, either completed or nearly completed, have been quite strikingly sexual.

ROBERT BLY was born in Minnesota in 1926. He has lived for various times in New York, in England, and in Scandinavia. In 1958 he launched *The Fifties,* which became *The Sixties* and *The Seventies*. He introduced the poets of his generation to many poets otherwise unknown such as Neruda, Vallejo, Tranströmer, Kabir, Machado, and Ponge. His recent books include *Morning Poems* (HarperCollins, 1977) and *Eating the Honey of Words: New and Selected Poems* (HarperCollins, 1999). Also in 1999 he published, in collaboration with Sunil Dutta, a volume of poems by the nineteenth-century Indian poet Ghalib under the title *The Lightning Should Have Fallen on Ghalib* (Ecco/HarperCollins). The poem included here is from his new book of poems, *The Night Abraham Called to the Stars,* which was published in May by HarperCollins. He was the guest editor of *The Best American Poetry 1999*.

Of "The French Generals," Bly writes: "After I looked at 'The French Generals' for a while, I decided the poem probably amounts to a meditation on the word 'many.' Napoleon, lying in his moist Elba bed, appears in it, just to throw you off. Those who follow every detail in a poem to its source are sure to be left behind in Elba. The mood of the poem is influenced by my admiration for the ghazals of Ghalib and Hafez in which there is no straight thread through the poem and each stanza can be read as a separate poem. Where the poem as a whole is going is a problem that the reader has to solve. I notice this poem has too many plural nouns in it, but perhaps one can forgive that because it's a poem about 'many.' I published an earlier version of the poem in the *TLS* under a different title. David Lehman has asked me to set down that version here as well. It seems that Jesus got into the title instead of Napoleon."

JESUS AT THE WELL

Whenever Jesus appears at the murky well,
I am waiting with my five hundred husbands.
It takes him all day to mention their names.

The growing soul longs for mastery, but
The small men inside pull it into misery.
It is the nature of shame to have many children.

We love our dark, greedy home. The serpent
Sends out his split tongue and waves it
In the air scented with many dark Napoleons.

The general goes to live in a small cottage
With damp sheets and useless French franc notes;
He keeps his old plans of attack under the mattress.

This world we love is the serpent's house.
We bring in newspapers to make his nest cozy.
It's the nature of wanting to have many wives.

So many rafters in lifejackets are pulled down
Till their toes touch the bottom of the Rogue River.
Wherever there is water there is someone drowning.

LEE ANN BROWN was born October 11, 1963, at Johnson Air Force Base, Saitama-ken, Japan. She was raised in Charlotte, North Carolina, and now resides in New York City. She is the author of *Polyverse* (Sun & Moon Press, 1999), which won the 1996 New American Poetry Series

Competition, and *The Sleep That Changed Everything,* forthcoming from Wesleyan University Press. She is the editor and publisher of Tender Buttons, a press that features experimental women's poetry. She received an M.F.A. in creative writing from Brown University in 1993 and has received fellowships from the New York Foundation for the Arts and the Fund for Poetry. She is currently an associate of Bard College's Institute for Writing and Thinking and an assistant professor of English at St. John's University.

Of "Sonnet Around Stephanie," Brown writes: "This poem was written upon hearing of the suicide of my girlhood friend, Stephanie Harrison, whom I had seen a few months before her death, in 1987. Elizabeth Robinson liked the poem and published a version of it in her Providence-based poetry newsletter, *Cold Water Business,* named for Lorine Niedecker's line. I pulled the poem out again in the past year as I was writing my second collection, which contains a number of elegies."

MICHAEL BURKARD was born in Rome, New York, in 1947. He currently teaches in the M.F.A. program at Syracuse University and in the summer program at the Fine Arts Work Center in Provincetown, where he also participated in MAKE: POEM, a showing of writer's drawings and paintings at the Schoolhouse Center for the Arts, and The C-Scape Mapping Project. He has taught in the past at Sarah Lawrence College and the University of Louisville, among other colleges, and has also worked as a psychiatric aide, an alcoholism and addictions counselor, and a proofreader for Bloomingdale's catalogues. He has been writing songs for many years. His books of poetry include *Unsleeping* (Sarabande Books, 2001), *Pennsylvania Collection Agency* (New Issues Press, 2001), *Entire Dilemma* (Sarabande Books, 1998), *My Secret Boat* (W. W. Norton, 1990), *Fictions from the Self* (W. W. Norton, 1988), *The Fires They Kept* (Metro Book Co., 1986), *Ruby for Grief* (University of Pittsburgh, 1981), *None, River* (Ironwood, 1979) and *In a White Light* (L'Epervier, 1977). He received two fellowships from the National Endowment for the Arts, two grants in poetry from the New York Foundation for the Arts, and, in 1988, a Whiting Writer's Award. Recent poems have appeared in *American Poetry Review, Fence, 3rd Bed,* and *Jubilat.* He is married to the artist Mary Alice Johnston.

Of "Notes About My Face," Burkard writes: "I wrote the poem in May of 1998; partly because of the fragments in the sequence I did not get much of a feel for what I had written for quite a while. I wrote into #7 and then returned to the poem the next day. A few of the fragments in #s 1–6 came from scattered notes. Except for this somewhat arbitrary reaching, I was improvising. The poem took more timing in #7—Jean Valentine had sent me a copy of a manuscript in progress and I had spent much very interested time with it. Her poems triggered a thought that I could turn to the reading event #7 talks to. And there had been a terrible brutal murder in New York City: the bodies of two young boys had just been discovered. I felt feeble beside this. I also wondered about some of the origins of my own wanting to write poetry, reasons for, perhaps suspect of . . . the pressures of school early on, later on . . . many different sources started crossing the poem perhaps as a way of using other art and poetry and poets as bridges, and some implicit admission that I am often much more comfortable and more truly my face with fragments from here and there without too much of a context. And wanting to state more of my political face? I looked at the notes a few times during the next year or so, and somewhere in 1999 the improvisation really began beckoning. I recopied it."

TRENT BUSCH was born in Brohard, West Virginia, in 1937. He has lived in Georgia for the past thirty years and owns a small place out in the country where he writes poetry and makes furniture. His poems have appeared in *Poetry, The Nation, Hudson Review, North American Review, Kenyon Review, Shenandoah, American Scholar,* and elsewhere. He is just now completing a book of poems entitled *Cuts from the Shop Floor.*

Of "Heartland," Busch writes: "If I could have heard half of what the woman says in this poem, I would be a little more qualified to speak about it. I have been involved in one way or another with farming all my life. One day being driven past a small house, long barns, and green tractors, I felt relieved they did not belong to me. I said so to my friend who was driving. Later, I wrote this poem about the couple we passed there."

AMINA CALIL was born in Stockton, California, in 1970. She lives in Oakland and Bangkok, and makes her living as a gardener and a midwife.

Of "Blouse of Felt," Calil writes, "After midnight, Schubert to play just a bit longer in the adjoining room his scofflaw narratives of children romping in metropolitan parks, I placed a massive picture book of plant forms on my lap, turned very slowly through its pages, and seemed to overhear 'Blouse of Felt' from the entities depicted there, and from those still active in my yard and body. The tones derive from psychic dilation. I am indebted to Flavor Flav for some of the cadences."

ANNE CARSON was born in Toronto, Canada, in 1950. She is a professor of classics at McGill University and has also taught recently at the University of Michigan and at Berkeley. Her books include *Glass, Irony and God* and *Men in the Off Hours* (Knopf, 2000). Her most recent book is *The Beauty of the Husband* (Knopf, 2001). She has received a Guggenheim Fellowship. Her work appears in *The Best of the Best American Poetry, 1988–1997*, edited by Harold Bloom. An article about Carson appeared in the *New York Times Magazine* in March 2000. "I'm conserving the past—it's what classicists are supposed to do," Carson told the reporter. "But there are ways to conserve it. One way is to say 'Nothing new is any good.' But you don't learn anything when you're still up on the window ledge, safe. The other way is to jump from what you know into empty space and see where you end up. I think you only learn things when you jump."

JOSHUA CLOVER was born in Berkeley, California, in 1962.

Of "Ceriserie," Clover writes: "While writing this poem I listened to 'Reasons To Be Beautiful' and 'Boys on the Radio' by Hole, 'The Everlasting' by Manic Street Preachers, 'Teardrop' by Massive Attack, 'Are You Still Mad?' and 'So Pure' by Alanis Morissette, 'Stolen Car' and 'Central Reservation (The Then Again Version)' by Beth Orton, and 'My Brother and Me' by Bruce Robison."

BILLY COLLINS was born in New York City in 1941. His books of poetry include *Picnic, Lightning* (University of Pittsburgh Press, 1998); *The Art of Drowning* (University of Pittsburgh Press, 1995), a finalist for the Lenore Marshall Poetry Prize; and *Questions About Angels* (William Morrow, 1991), which was selected by Edward Hirsch for the National Poetry Series and was reprinted by the University of Pittsburgh Press in 1999. This year Random House will publish his new and selected poems, *Sailing Alone Around the Room*. He has won the Bess Hokin Prize, the Frederick Bock Prize, the Oscar Blumenthal Prize, and the Levinson Prize—all awarded by *Poetry* magazine. A recipient of a Guggenheim Fellowship and a grant from the National Endowment for the Arts, he is a professor of English at Lehman College (City University of New York) and a visiting writer at Sarah Lawrence College. He lives in northern Westchester County. His poems have appeared in the 1992 and 1993 editions of *The Best American Poetry* and in each of the last four books in this series.

Of "Snow Day," Collins writes: "Long since recovered from the trance of writing this poem, I now have an outsider's view of it, which enables me to see all sorts of things that had little or nothing to do with its composition. For example, I see the poem as a series of steps that take us from a collective experience to a private one. The poem begins with the public event of snow (which Joyce would describe as 'general') and ends with three imagined girls whispering secrets. First, we are offered a kind of Marxist notion of snow as having the power to subvert civic life. Then we move to the domestic scene of speaker, tea, dog, radio. The poem gets strangely bogged down in the names of closed schools (all of which were lifted from the Yellow Pages), which leads us to a playground and finally into an intimate circle of conspiratorial little girls. In Chinese poetry this technique is called 'The Shepherd' because figuratively you begin with a widely dispersed flock and end in the enclosure of a sheepfold. If I step back further, I might say that a possible grandfather to this poem is Coleridge's 'Frost at Midnight' with its similar attention to winter and childhood. But if I took another step backwards, I might trip over a piece of furniture."

ROBERT CREELEY born in 1926, is a New Englander by birth and disposition although he has spent much of his life in other parts of the world, including Guatemala, British Columbia, France, and Spain. In the 1950s he taught at Black Mountain College and edited *The Black Mountain Review.* In 1966 he began teaching at the State University of New York in Buffalo. *For Love, Windows,* and *Selected Poems* are among his collections of poetry. He has also written a novel (*The Island*) and a collection of stories (*The Gold Diggers*).

Of "En Famille," Creeley writes: "This poem was written expressly for a collaboration with the photographer Elsa Dorfman. In fact, you can see what came of it at this site: http:// www.granarybooks.com/ books/dorfman/dorfman2.html.

It all began when Ellie gave me a great batch of her portraits—from which I first made a selection of ten for the so-called narrative of the poem, then an additional six for either end, making twelve—so twenty-two in all. I was up in Maine by myself, and I put the whole sequence on our big kitchen table, and then just sat and looked at them. Outside our place there's a big hayfield sloping down, with woods going off on all sides. I guess that's how Wordsworth got in there, with that opening line—and then, later, the wind. I would write two quatrains for each portrait, then move to the next—closing with old friend Bill Alfred's wise look (now gone, alas) and his dear friend Faye Dunaway. Perhaps because I was alone there, these dear people all became my company. They certainly made me recognize that I, like all, much needed it."

LYDIA DAVIS was born in Northampton, Massachusetts, in 1947. She is the author of *The Thirteenth Woman* (Living Hand Editions, 1976), *Sketches for a Life of Wassilly* (Station Hill Press, 1981), *Story and Other Stories* (The Figures, 1983), *Break It Down* (Farrar, Straus and Giroux, 1986), *The End of the Story* (Farrar, Straus and Giroux, 1995), and *Almost No Memory* (Farrar, Straus and Giroux, 1997). She has also translated numerous books from the French, including works by Maurice Blanchot, Michel Leiris, and Pierre-Jean Jouve. Her translation of Proust's *Swann's Way* will be published by Penguin UK in 2002. She lives in upstate New York.

Of "A Mown Lawn," Davis writes: "Towns lawns all mown, some poisoned, all free of weeds, all free of cover, some planned plantings, no loose small animals, no loose insects, some pets, some penned dogs, some tied and housed dogs, some pests, in effigy: effigy of raccoon, effigy of deer, effigy of Canada goose (no nibbling, no nuisance, no ruin of planned plantings), unmoving goose flock feed on poisoned mown lawn, red bows on necks come holiday."

R. ERICA DOYLE was born in Brooklyn, New York, in 1968 to Trinidadian parents. Her work has appeared in *Callaloo, Ms. Magazine, Black Issues Book Review, Blithe House Quarterly,* and *Sinister Wisdom,* and is forthcoming in the anthology *Other Countries: Voices Rising.* She received her M.F.A. in poetry from the New School in New York City. While living in Washington, DC, for twelve years, she taught creative writing and developed literacy curricula for young children at Children's Studio School; taught community writing workshops; and worked as a lesbian peer counselor, a paralegal, and a domestic violence activist. She has received grants and awards from the DC Commission on the Arts and Humanities and the Humanities Council of DC, and is a fellow of Cave Canem: A Retreat and Workshop for African. American Poets. She lives with her partner in Tel Aviv, Israel.

Of "Ma Ramon," Doyle writes: "My great-grandmother was a mean and manipulative person, and I wrote this poem as the antithesis and antidote to every 'grandmother' poem I'd ever read. She was the most singularly influential person in our family; her iron will, deviousness, tyranny, arrogance, and generosity are legendary, the ties she created still existent. Using the fragments of our family's oral history I pieced together a portrait of an ancestor who intrigued me as much for her political being as for her position in the histories as an emotional or nostalgic figure. Her machinations seemed to be as much a function of her will and personality as they were essential for her survival and, ultimately, success. She was a person who occupied multiple linguistic, geographic, legal, temporal, and cultural spaces and who operated, at least at the beginning of her life, from a position where her only privilege was the color of her fair skin. In the process of putting the pieces of her story together I saw a 'w/hole' that the great leveler of archetypal American popular culture was intent on erasing, given its inability to handle complexity and the tendency to romanticize a cruel past. She embodies the betweenness I carry within myself, a habitual and existential multiplicity."

CHRISTOPHER EDGAR was born in Pasadena, California, in 1961. His poems have appeared in *The Germ, Shiny, Lincoln Center Theater Review, The Portable Boog Reader,* and *The Best American Poetry 2000,* and he won the 2000 *Boston Review* poetry prize. An editor of *The Hat,* a literary magazine, Edgar is the translator of *Tolstoy as Teacher: Leo Tolstoy's Writings on Education* (Teachers & Writers Collaborative, 2000) and has coedited a number of books on teaching writing, including *Classics in the Classroom: Using Great Literature to Teach Writing* (Teachers & Writers Collaborative, 1999). He is publications director of Teachers & Writers Collaborative, a nonprofit arts organization in New York City, where he lives.

Of "The Cloud of Unknowing," Edgar writes: "I have always liked poems about travel, especially those of Valéry Larbaud, Blaise Cendrars, and Kenneth Koch. One day I was thinking about writing a poem about travel. I gazed dumbly at the bookshelf waiting for something to happen when *The Cloud of Unknowing* popped out from among the other spines. The central idea of this book, a treatise on knowledge by medieval English mystics, is (crudely) that in order to see one must first blur one's vision for a time. This seemed like something I could use, so I went with it, and wrote the rest of the poem without stopping. The events and places in the poem are mostly, but not all, from my own experience—a few are made up or lifted from others' accounts. The particular details weren't so important to me, though; I wanted to write a poem of many parts in one continuous zigzagging segue to approximate the experience of travel. Losing one's way, and having the freedom to do so, is a real pleasure, and when one feels relatively weightless—at sea in a port town or in a poem by Pierre Reverdy—a certain sense of recognition is sometimes heightened. Ending the poem in Heathrow seemed appropriate, since it's sort of a way station between Old and New Worlds, between our current, homogenized, post-International-style world and what came before."

THOMAS SAYERS ELLIS—or Sayers (after Gale) as he is known to family and friends—was born in Washington, DC, in 1963. Educated at Harvard University and Brown University, where he earned the M.F.A. in 1995, he is the author of *The Good Junk* (Take Three, Graywolf, 1996) and a chapbook, *The Genuine Negro Hero* (Kent State University Press, 2001). His poems have most recently appeared in *Giant Steps: The New Generation of American Writers; The New Young American Poets; American Poetry: The Next Generation,* and *The New American Poets: A Breadloaf Anthology.* A member of the core faculty of the Bennington Writing Seminars, he currently resides in Cleveland, Ohio, where he is an assistant professor of English at Case Western Reserve University.

Ellis writes: "I began 'T.A.P.O.A.F.O.M.' as a celebration and exploration of crossed and not yet crossed crossroads at Yaddo in the Nipple Room (West House), where Phillip Roth wrote *The Breast,* and I finished it in a park in Cleveland, Ohio, only days before Parliament-Funkadelic, a.k.a. P-Funk, was inducted into the Rock and Roll Hall of Fame. I wanted to write a poem for *That Fuss Was Us,* whose content and structure demonstrated the many nuances of difficulty I had witnessed navigating the languages and styles of form and formlessness, fake-ass freedom, between funky and unfunky worlds, and one that would juxtapose the twentieth anniversary of the landing of P-Funk's mothership with the tenth anniversary of The Dark Room Collective, which was officially founded the minute I met Sharán Strange. In the poem, I am working on my own brand of literary activism, which I call Genuine Negro Heroism. Genuine Negro Heroism (GNH) is the opposite of HNIC (Head Negro In Charge), and incorporates pee-pure modes of black freak, black folk, and black soul behavior such as signifying, shouting out, cursing, and playing the double-mouthed dozens like 'Yo momma ate-out Coretta Scott King, and got Ralph Abernathy on her chin.'

"I also intended for 'T.A.P.O.A.F.O.M.' to have three sections instead of two and to be the first poem with an afterparty. Regrettably, 'Afterparty' wouldn't surrender. Run and tell it like you run and tell everything else."

AMY ENGLAND was born in Alamorgordo, New Mexico, in 1962, and grew up in Illinois. She taught English as a second language in Tokyo and Chicago, and received a Ph.D. in creative writing from the University of Denver. Her first book of poems, *The Flute Ship Castricum*, was released by Tupelo Press in April of 2001. She edits Transparent Tiger Press, which publishes poetry chapbooks, and will be a visiting lecturer next year in Naropa University's writing and literature program.

England writes: "I've always been interested in the line that divides poetry from prose. 'The Art of the Snake Story' is the culminating piece in a manuscript *Victory and Her Opposites: a Guide,* which explores this division; the nominal subject is an archeological site in Greece. In doing research on this excavation and the history of the cult that was practiced there, I repeatedly came across images of snakes, which gave me the idea of combining a poem about the significance of those images with stories people had told me. I would like here to thank the sources of these stories: Eric Elshtain, Matthew Michael, Jim Bequette, Carol Loftin, Valerie Leppert, Barrett Shukla, and Carmen Curton."

ALAN FELDMAN was born in New York City in 1945. As an undergraduate at Columbia he edited *Columbia Review;* Columbia Review Press published his book of poems, *The Household* (1966). His second collection, *The Happy Genius* (SUN, 1978), won the annual Elliston Book Award for the best book of poems by an independent press in the United States. *The Personals,* a chapbook, came out in 1982, and *Anniversary,* self-published with color drawings by his wife, Nan Hass Feldman, in 1992. He is a professor of English at Framingham State College and also teaches writing at the Radcliffe Seminars, Harvard University. His most recent book, *State College 101: A Freshman Writing Class,* (www.xlibris.com), is about the "ignored middle"—working-class suburban kids who are first-generation college students—and the efforts of his colleague, professor Elaine Beilin, to educate them.

Feldman writes: "I wrote 'Contemporary American Poetry' immediately after delivering a visiting lecture on contemporary poetry at a Radcliffe Seminar. Some of the students were almost ninety, and they were finishing a two-year survey of great books. To prepare for me, they'd each brought a recent poem they liked. I kept thinking how perfectly my mother would have fit into such a group; like them she was well read, receptive, but (in a healthy way) somewhat skeptical, too. When she sent me Donald Hall's 'Kicking the Leaves' years ago, I didn't want to admire the poem. I felt my mother had gone over to the enemy. As a fan of New York poets Kenneth Koch and Frank O'Hara, I believed that poems could be more moving by being funny. Since then,

whatever schism in American poetry this represented must have l
When my poem appeared in *Poetry,* I received a gracious letter fror
saying how much it pleased him. He reads it as being in-tune wi
poem (different as the styles may be) and, I hope, as a tribute.

"My mother died in 1976, more than twenty years before I taught that poetry class. I don't claim to commune with spirits, but she can speak to me the way fictional characters do, dictating her own dialogue, which is what she began to do. Does she really believe that being 'troubled' is essential to the making of a poet, or is she just making excuses for me, thinking I should have devoted myself to poetry more single-mindedly? Though simpler than it was when she was alive, ours is still a loving but complicated relationship."

JAMES GALVIN was born in Chicago in May 1951. He teaches in the University of Iowa Writers' Workshop. He is the author of *The Meadow* and *Fencing the Sky* (both from Holt) and *Resurrection Update* (Copper Canyon Press). His earlier books include *God's Mistress* (Harper & Row) in 1984 and *Elements* (Copper Canyon Press) in 1988.

LOUISE GLÜCK was born in New York City in 1943. She is the author of ten books of poetry including, most recently, *The Seven Ages* (Ecco/HarperCollins, 2001). She received the National Book Critics Circle Award in poetry for *The Triumph of Achilles* (Ecco, 1985) and the Pulitzer Prize for *The Wild Iris* (Ecco, 1992). Her other poetry volumes include *Firstborn* (1968), *The House on Marshland* (1975), *The Garden* (1976), *Descending Figure* (1980), *Ararat* (1990), *Meadowlands* (1996), and *Vita Nova* (1999). A prose book, *Proofs and Theories: Essays on Poetry,* appeared in 1994. She has taught at Williams College since 1984. She received the Bollingen Prize in 2001. She was guest editor of *The Best American Poetry 1993.*

"My compositional process," Glück told Brian Phillips, who interviewed her in 1999, "almost always begins in a kind of despondency, or hopelessness, or desolation, usually born of a conviction that I will never write again. That I will at long intervals turn out little mechanical B+ poems, but that I'll never again feel that I am at the throat of the dog, that I'm at something essential. This pattern really hasn't varied, though my first book was more diligently written. But even then there were long hiatuses of silence and periods of despondency, life in the desert, that have come to seem to me the norm of my aesthetic life . . . which isn't to say those passages are not brutal. So that each of my books really begins with a prayer, you know: Appear to me again. Let me be suffused with the wish to, and ability to, make meaning out of language."

JEWELLE GOMEZ was born in Boston, Massachusetts, in 1948. A novelist, poet, and essayist, she makes her living as an administrator for arts and philanthropic organizations. She is the author of six books, including three collections of poetry. *The Gilda Stories* (Firebrand Books, 1991), a novel, was the winner of two Lambda Literary Awards, for fiction and science fiction. A recent collection of short stories, *Don't Explain* (Firebrand Books) appeared in 1999.

Gomez writes: "Whenever I read 'My Chakabuku Mama' it always gets uproarious laughter of recognition from people who identify with either the smugly self-righteous partner or with the puzzled, eager innocent who gets left behind. I love the response, but I always find the poem a bit sad because of the betrayal it represents. While it is a story told about a romance, to me it embodies many other types of exploitative relationships, especially between U.S. workers and corporate entities, or between lecturers and academic institutions, or between consumers and manufacturers. The personal is political, always."

JORIE GRAHAM was born in New York City in 1950. She grew up in Italy, studied in French schools, and attended the Sorbonne, New York University, Columbia University, and the University of Iowa. Her most recent collections of poetry are *The Dream of the Unified Field: Selected Poems 1974–1994* (Ecco, 1995), for which she received the Pulitzer Prize; *The Errancy* (Ecco/HarperCollins, 1998); and *Swarm* (Ecco/HarperCollins, 2000). A new collection, titled *Never,* is forthcoming in spring 2002. She is currently Boylston Professor at Harvard University. A MacArthur Fellow, she was the guest editor of *The Best American Poetry 1990.*

Of "Gulls," Graham writes: "The poem so evidently *is* what it *does,* it doesn't seem to require much explication. It attempts an acute act of description, tries to enact the emotional and spiritual states awakened thereby, and, finally, turns 'back' on those two 'first acts' in a final motion into meditation. It feels like an act of self-portraiture. It was, in its first draft, written *en plein air*—not unlike how painters, especially those of the Romantic period, happily place their easels and painting-boxes 'out' in 'nature.' It is, of course, in the trawling of such actions 'inside' (as well as 'indoors') that the problem of subjectivity—with which the poem, in its attempts at objectivity, is so strenuously involved—is brought into focus. It feels moving and urgent, as a process, to me. As I undertake it, sitting on the shore, peering intently, pen in hand, it feels like all the human history of inwardness is recapitulating itself in such attempted acts of representation. Then it just turns into a poem again and I really don't know much about it, except how vividly the wind came up as the sun went down."

LINDA GREGERSON was born in Elgin, Illinois, in 1950, and was educated at Oberlin College, the University of Iowa, and Stanford University. Her most recent book of poems, *The Woman Who Died in Her Sleep* (Houghton Mifflin, 1996), was a finalist for both the Poets' Prize and the Lenore Marshall Award. She is also the author of *Fire in the Conservatory* (Dragon Gate, 1982), *The Reformation of the Subject* (Cambridge University Press, 1995), and *Negative Capability: Contemporary American Poetry* (University of Michigan Press, 2001). Her third book of poems, *Waterborne,* will be published by Houghton Mifflin in 2002. Gregerson has received the Levinson Prize from *Poetry* magazine, the Consuelo Ford Award from the Poetry Society of America, the Isabel MacCaffrey Award from the Spenser Society of America, and a Guggenheim Fellowship. She teaches Renaissance literature and creative writing at the University of Michigan.

Of "Waterborne," Gregerson writes: "I am capable of shameful oblivion toward the world around me, especially the world of nature, but the dawn mists that gather on the surface of the Huron River in the spring and fall are the loveliest thing I see all day. Why those seasons in particular? Something to do with the temperature differentials between the water and the air? Thank heaven there are people who know more about these things than I do. And about bridge building (ours is quite decrepit; the school buses are no longer allowed to cross it) and the drainage of cornfields. I took a liberty in section two, omitting to mention that the river in question has temporarily metamorphosed into the Wisconsin River, some sixty miles north of Madison, where my uncle Gordon and my father and their siblings grew up. My neighbor tells me he'll take carp or walleye when he can't get bass, and he didn't take me for an agent of the DNR when I pulled over to ask."

LINDA GREGG was born in Suffern, New York, in 1942. Her fifth book of poems, *Things and Flesh,* was published by Graywolf Press in 1999. Her first two books, *Too Bright to See* and *Alma,* will be republished jointly in fall 2001. Also, this fall she is teaching at Princeton University. She currently lives in New York City.

Of "The Singers Change, The Music Goes On," Gregg writes: "This poem is trying to make a whole out of a contradiction. The permanence in myths, shards, temples and song, but also the permanence that was lived in the body and place. Love and revelations. Lasting, because of its heartbreaking momentariness."

ALLEN GROSSMAN was born in Minneapolis, Minnesota, in 1932. His most recent publications are *The Ether Dome* (1991), *The Philosopher's Window* (1995) and *How to Do Things with Tears* (2001), all available from New Directions. *The Long Schoolroom: Lessons in the Bitter Logic of the Poetic Principle* was published by the University of Michigan Press in 1997. He is the Mellon Professor in the Humanities at Johns Hopkins University.

Of "Enough rain for Agnes Walquist," Grossman writes: " 'Agnes' was the first name I ever knew. Her body was the first body I could name. I could think, 'Agnes is here' or I could think, 'Agnes is not here.' I have thought for most of a long life, 'Agnes is not here.' Agnes is, herself, the beginning and the end of my memory. I remember because she remembered. What she remembered I remember—as it happened, the sound of night rain.

"Some months ago I found a postal envelope among some other papers thrown away but not quite lost. It was addressed by my mother to Agnes Walquist. The envelope was empty. So I could make a poem for that envelope empty otherwise and send it off, the action of gratitude, making remembered in the world what she remembered. Remember what she remembered.

"All the names in this poem and in the book of which this poem is a part (*How to Do Things with Tears*) are like this."

DONALD HALL was born in New Haven, Connecticut, on September 20, 1928. He has earned his living as a freelance writer since 1975, the year he moved to a family farm in New Hampshire with his wife, the late poet Jane Kenyon. He had previously held a tenured professorship at the University of Michigan. He initiated Michigan's "Poets on Poetry" and "Under Discussion" series and served as the general editor of both until 1994. His recent books of poetry include *The One Day* (1988), which won the National Book Critics Circle Award; *Old and New Poems* (1990), *The Museum of Clear Ideas* (1992), *The Old Life* (1995) and

Without (1998), all published by Houghton Mifflin. A new volume entitled *The Painted Bed* expected in 2002. He was the guest editor of *The Best American Poetry 1989*.

Of "Her Garden," Hall writes: "For more than forty years Thomas Hardy has been one of my favorite poets in the language. But I never thought of trying to write the kind of stanza in which he often wrote: irregular lengths of iambic, all rhyming; the prosodic scheme repeated in further stanzas.

"Some of Hardy's best poems derive from the death of his first wife—a marriage which does not resemble Jane's and mine—and I don't believe I adopted his stanza because of subject matter. In the spring of 1998 I surprised myself by beginning to write these Hardyish poems, of which 'Her Garden' is the second. Stanzaic poems take much less time and effort, fewer drafts, than poems in free verse. The net determines some properties of the shot in tennis; free verse requires a net but its net is arbitrary. I continue to write free verse."

ANTHONY HECHT was born in New York City in 1923. He received the Pulitzer Prize in poetry in 1968, the Bollingen Prize in 1983, the Wallace Stevens Award from the Academy of American Poets in 1999, and the Robert Frost Medal in 2000. Among his published books are *Collected Earlier Poems* (Knopf, 1990), *The Transparent Man* (Knopf, 1990), *On the Laws of the Poetic Art* (Princeton), and *The Hidden Law: The Poetry of W. H. Auden* (Harvard, 1981). He lives in Washington, DC.

Of "Sarabande on Attaining the Age of Seventy-Seven," Hecht writes: "When I was twenty-nine, I read in an anthology, *A Little Treasury of Modern Poetry,* edited by Oscar Williams, a poem by George Santayana called "Minuet on Reaching the Age of Fifty." It began:

> Old age, on tiptoe, lays her jewelled hand
> Lightly on mine.—Come, tread a stately measure
> Most gracious partner, nobly posed and bland.
>   Ours be no boisterous pleasure . . . .

I'm sure that at twenty-nine, fifty must have seemed very elderly, and I had a number of white-haired aunts whose jewels could not divert my glance from the large, worming blood vessels in their hands. There was something vaguely Spenserian about Santayana's poem, with its personifications and inverted word orders and dated vocabulary. Nevertheless, it had a certain charm that I recalled when I was far older than Santayana when he wrote it. The idea of a solitary dance (the sarabande can be danced alone) seemed right for someone my age, and without any further reference to Santayana's poem I set off to write one for myself. Moreover, I am not a good dancer, and the better for dancing alone."

LYN HEJINIAN was born in the San Francisco Bay Area in 1941 and lives in Berkeley. Her books include *My Life* (1987), *The Cell* (1992), and *The Cold of Poetry* (1994), all from Sun & Moon Press. The University of California Press has just published a collection of her essays entitled *The Language of Inquiry*. She has collaborated on projects with many poets and artists, among them Leslie Scalapino, Michael Davidson, Ron Silliman, and Barrett Watten. In 2000 she received the fellowship of the Academy of American Poets.

Hejinian writes: "The group of short poems entitled 'Nights' is part of a long-term project, a collection of night thoughts intended as an homage to Scheherazade. The work in its entirety is meant to give an account of nocturnal adventures, most of them entirely imaginary. These adventures take the form of somniloquys, insomniac lyrics, lullabies, fables, ghost stories, etc., and involve nighttime philosophizing, fretting, hallucinations, fantasies, eroticism, dreams, fear, and nonsense. The nonsense in question erupts with dark hilarity and is often ominous."

BRENDA HILLMAN was born in Tucson, Arizona, in 1951. She serves on the faculty of Saint Mary's College in Moraga, California. Her six collections of poetry—*White Dress* (1985), *Fortress* (1989), *Death Tractates* (1992), *Bright Existence* (1993), *Loose Sugar* (1997), and *Cascadia* (2001) are from Wesleyan University Press; she has also written three chapbooks, *Coffee, 3 AM* (Penumbra Press, 1982), *Autumn Sojourn* (Em Press, 1995), and *The Firecage* (a+bend press, 2000). Hillman has edited an edition of Emily Dickinson's poetry for Shambhala Publications, and, with Patricia Dienstfrey, has coedited *New Writings on Poetics and Motherhood*.

Of "The Formation of Soils," Hillman writes: "The strata in this poem are wide, mobile, soft, as when the story had been restless but isn't anymore. I was thinking about the making of soil in the middle of a state, as distinct from the making of dirt. In relation to something like an era, love or insight seems like air, and human times of making (or, as we sometimes say, *having*) experiences are so brief compared to how long it takes for rocks to crumble. All the kinds of significance are layered in an unknown order."

JANE HIRSHFIELD was born in New York City in 1953. She is the author of five collections of poetry, most recently *Given Sugar, Given Salt* (HarperCollins, 2001). Her other books include a collection of essays, *Nine Gates: Entering the Mind of Poetry,* and two anthologies collecting the work of women poets from the past. She has received fellowships from the Guggenheim and Rockefeller foundations, the Poetry Center Book Award, the Bay Area Book Reviewers Award, and other honors. This is her second appearance in the *Best American Poetry* series. A resident of the San Francisco Bay Area, she teaches in the low-residency Bennington MFA Writing Seminars.

Of "In Praise of Coldness," Hirshfield writes: "It has long seemed to me that one of the defining qualities in a human life is the tension between the path of the passions and that of a certain nonattachment to one's own fate. The advice the poem quotes (from one of Chekhov's letters) strikes me as somehow related to a solution 'If you want to move your reader, write more coldly.' The underbelly of that sentence is what interests: the point is not the coldness, but the way that a restraining coldness can in fact contain heat, can move the reader more than would a simple explosive outpouring. In art, in life, a certain coldness (the emotional distance of classical tragedy, the technical use of perspective in a Renaissance canvas, the capacity a person might have to step back sometimes from the pulses' racing) allows, paradoxically, greater feeling, greater range, increase of compassion, but it cannot so dominate as to deny human feeling, human life. Heat alone is narcissism; coldness alone is fatal. And so a dying man daydreams of travel, of eating, knowing all the while that he dreams the contemplation of Chekhov's allegiance to the world of the living, right to the end, both breaks and awakens the heart.

"The Japanese call the human realm 'the world of the middle,' or 'the world of betweenness.' One task then of a human life is to find a way of being that seats itself between—that falls neither into a plummeting, arid coldness nor into unrestrained heat. (It is only because we humans lean by nature toward warmth that the title of this poem leans toward the cold.) What I've written here, I must add, are the thoughts that came to mind while looking at the poem in retrospect. In writing it, one line simply followed the next onto the page, and I only discovered in the reading and revising of those lines what the poem was exploring in its words and musics. That discovering, and its consequent clarifying, are the reason I write."

JOHN HOLLANDER was born in New York City in 1929. He has published eighteen books of poetry, the most recent being *Figurehead* (Knopf, 1999) and a reissue with added notes and commentary of his *Reflections on Espionage* (Yale University Press, 1999). He has also published several books of criticism and theory, most recently *The Work of Poetry* (Columbia University Press, 1997) and *The Poetry of Everyday Life* (University of Michigan Press, 1998). Among the awards he has received for his work are the Bollingen Prize, the Levinson Prize, and a MacArthur Fellowship. He lives in Connecticut and is Sterling Professor of English at Yale University. He was the guest editor of *The Best American Poetry 1998*.

Of "What the Lovers in the Old Songs Thought," Hollander writes: "In this bit of play with the poetry of love (love-poetry, love-making, love's made-up stories about itself) I took up a form of story about Origins that had puzzled me since later childhood, the opening of the Fourth Gospel: 'In the beginning was the Word, and the Word was with God, and the Word was God.' Before I knew what the *Logos* might be, I'd puzzled at how something that was *with* something else might be said to be identical to what it was with. (Not being a Christian, I had had no educational guidance in the matter.) In college, I came across Faust's great sequence of revisions (and, finally, Trotsky's footnote to the last revision. 'In the Beginning was the Deed. The word followed as its phonetic shadow.'). My feelings about the revisionary sequence, and about claims of origination in religion, poetry, and love, found their place in this poem."

RICHARD HOWARD was born in Cleveland, Ohio, in 1929. He was educated at Columbia University and the Sorbonne. The most recent of his eleven books of poems is *Trappings* (Turtle Point Press, 1999); for his third, *Untitled Subjects,* he was awarded the Pulitzer Prize in 1970. He has translated more than 150 works from the French, including Stendhal's *The Charterhouse of Parma* for the Modern Library, and he received the American Book Award for his translation of Baudelaire's *Les Fleurs du mal*. He is a member of the American Academy of Arts and Letters and served as the Poet Laureate of New York State from 1994 to 1995. In 1996 he was named a Fellow of the MacArthur Foundation. He is poetry editor of both *The Paris Review* and *Western Humanities Review,* and teaches in the writing division of the School of the Arts at Columbia University. A chancellor of the Academy of American Poets, he was guest editor of *The Best American Poetry 1995*.

Of "After 65," Howard writes: "The poem was published five years late—it was written for a project of 'Poets Then and Now' by photographer Rollie McKenna, who asked for a poem of comment on her images thirty years apart."

FANNY HOWE was born in Buffalo, New York, in 1940, and grew up in Boston. She is a professor of writing and American literature at the University of California, San Diego. Her most recent novels are *Nod* (Sun & Moon, 1998) and *Indivisible* (Semiotext(e)/MIT Press, 2001). Her most recent collections of poems are *One Crossed Out* (Graywolf, 1997) and *Selected Poems* (University of California Press, 2000).

Howe writes: " 'Doubt' was written for a conference on Simone Weil two years ago at Columbia University. I ended up reading poems instead, because the atmosphere was contentious. . . . Originally I thought of this as a lyrical essay, but increasingly *all* my writing tends toward poetry, including my most recent novel, *Indivisible*. I can no longer make distinctions between the genres. This must have developed naturally over time, though I think it always created a problem for my prose, which might have had a happier life if I had called it poetry."

OLENA KALYTIAK DAVIS was born in Detroit in 1963. Her first book, *And Her Soul Out of Nothing*, was published by the University of Wisconsin Press in 1997. Her work has recently been anthologized in *The New American Poets: A Breadloaf Anthology; American Poetry: The Next Generation; The Best American Poetry 2000;* and *Pushcart Prize XXV.* She is currently living in Alaska, raising a family, and slowly finishing her second manuscript, *Shattered Sonnets Love Card and Other Off and Back Handed Importunities.*

Kalytiak Davis writes: " 'Sweet Reader, Flanneled and Tulled' was inspired by the opening sentence of the final chapter of *Jane Eyre:* 'Reader, I married him.' Not only did I want that kind of intimate and immediate relationship with my reader, I wanted to see just how intimate and immediate 'we' could actually become. It took me a long time to figure it out, as is the case with any emotional/sexual pairing. Naturally, it turned into a love/hate thing.

"Following my usual method, I sought help, by which I mean blatantly stole, from numerous and miscellaneous sources ranging from Milton's description of the good angel Abdiel to "Nessmuk"'s *Woodcraft and Camping.* (Speaking of craft, this poem was intentionally crafted to be read aloud; I also remember at the time being interested in Allen Grossman's premise of repetition as the absence of rhyme.) I saved nothing when writing 'Sweet Reader . . .', I put everything in it including my hang-ups and infidelities, my tea and my crumpets. This was several years ago. I sometimes feel I still haven't restocked my mental or poetic arsenals. Then again, it could be all these babies I seem to be suddenly having. . . ."

SHIRLEY KAUFMAN was born in Seattle, lived in San Francisco, and has resided in Jerusalem since 1973. Among her seven books published in the United States are *The Floor Keeps Turning* (University of Pittsburgh Press, 1970), *Rivers of Salt* (Copper Canyon Press, 1993), and *Roots in the Air: New and Selected Poems* (Copper Canyon Press, 1996). She has also translated several volumes of Hebrew poetry by Israeli poets Abba Kovner, Amir Gilboa, and Meir Wieseltier (forthcoming, University of California Press); and also a selection of poems from the Dutch of Judith Herzberg. Kaufman's *Selected Poems,* translated into Hebrew by Dan Pagis and Aharon Shabtai, was published by the Bialik Press in Jerusalem in 1995.

Of "The Emperor of China," Kaufman writes: "This poem grew and kept changing for almost two years. I began it in a study-bedroom at Kresge College of the University of California at Santa Cruz, where I wrote every morning for a week in August, looking out the window at the sunlit forest and the proprietary deer nibbling at the shrubs and leaves. I thought I was writing about this dreamy California scene, but my home in Jerusalem immediately intruded (as it always does when I'm writing in the U.S.A.) together with the memory of our friend's eightieth birthday party a month earlier. I realized how much I was 'enjoying my life' at that very moment.

"When I write, my personal life is usually mixed up with political events, daily news, conversations, associative memories, and a range of sensory detail that often overwhelms me. I don't sort all this out while the words keep coming. I'm happy when the random images keep rolling faster than I can write them down. I'm not at all sure at such an early stage where they are going, and what they will mean in the end. When I discover that, often much later, I can begin to shape the poem. "When I returned to Israel, to the very different world where I live most of the time, there was another window, in my study facing the street, the flats and gardens across from me. I watched the first clouds come after a long blue summer. Always the man across the street is cleaning his garden and sweeping the stone path from the sidewalk to the door of his home with such obsessive compulsion that he must be crazy. Summer and winter in the same khaki shorts and sandals. In the winter he adds socks.

"There's a thin curtain blowing across my vision much of the time (especially now as I write this at the end of January 2001). So that acts of kindness, pleasure in spring and gardening, a children's choir, even love keep dissolving into unease, anger, sometimes fear—and memories of Kieslowski's film, or the Holocaust, or the Gulf War, every war. Human suffering takes over.

" 'The Peace and Other Dreams Writers' Conference' was really the name of that Beersheva University conference. It took me a long time to weave it all together."

GALWAY KINNELL was born in Providence, Rhode Island, in 1927. He received a B.A. at Princeton University and an M.A. at the University of Rochester. His early books include *The Book of Nightmares* (1971) and *The Avenue Bearing the Initial of Christ into the New World* (1974), both from Houghton Mifflin. He won the Pulitzer Prize in 1983. His most recent books are *The Essential Rilke,* translated with Hannah Liebmann (Ecco Press) and *A New Selected Poems* (Houghton Mifflin). He lives in Vermont and New York, where he teaches in the graduate writing program at New York University.

Of "The Quick and the Dead," Kinnell writes: "My one regret in witnessing the events that are recounted in the poem is that I didn't photograph the creatures involved, or measure them, for better identification later. But in fact I was so enthralled by the burial and by the arrival of the female and some spectators that identification was the last thing on my mind. When the drama was over I felt I had been present at something like a medieval miracle play. As for the uncommon words, I like inventing words, using words that are still ahead of us, but just as much I like trying to save some of those that are falling off behind us."

DAVID KIRBY was born in Baton Rouge, Louisiana, in 1944. He is currently the W. Guy McKenzie Professor of English at Florida State University. His poems appear in *The Best American Poetry 2000* and *Pushcart Prize 2001,* and his books of poetry include *Big-Leg Music* (1995), *My Twentieth Century* (1999), both from Orchives Press, and, most recently, *The House of Blue Light* (Louisiana State University Press, 2000). He is married to the poet Barbara Hamby and lives in Tallahassee, Florida.

Of "Dear Derrida," Kirby writes: "A lot of poets can't stand theory, but I guess I believe in everything. Or, as Picasso said, I don't care who influences me as long as it isn't myself.

"Actually, there is one problem with deconstruction, which is that it's a French idea that amounts to an all-out assault on the masterpiece-kissing educational system in that country. Over here, of course, we aren't all that well-constructed in the first place. After you've been through our public schools, you're not really weighed down with all this information that needs to be taken apart, so deconstruction is kind of silly for Americans.

"On the other hand, a little indeterminacy isn't a bad thing. When my friend decided to put that gun barrel in his mouth, I just wish he hadn't been so sure of himself."

CAROLYN KIZER was born in Spokane, Washington, in 1925, and was educated in Spokane public schools. Her father was a noted civil liberties lawyer and urban planner. She has three children and is married to John Marshall Woodbridge, FAIA, also a city planner. She graduated from Sarah Lawrence College in 1945, and then became a fellow of the Chinese government at Columbia University; she subsequently went to China, where her father directed Chinese relief. Founder of the poetry quarterly *Poetry Northwest,* she was the first director of literature for the National Endowment for the Arts. *Cool, Calm and Collected: Poems 1960–2000* has just been published by Copper Canyon Press. In 1985 she received the Pulitzer Prize in poetry for *Yin: New Poems* (BOA Editions, 1984). She lives in Sonoma, California, and part-time in Paris.

Of "The Ashes," Kizer writes: "Periodically, I circle back to China, where I first lived in 1947–48. Evidence of the coming revolution was everywhere, as was the corruption of the Kuomintang warlords and the misery of the common people. It was such a traumatic year that I've rarely been able to cope with the memories. This poem comes as close as anything I've written. It is dedicated to William Gass because he also attended a meeting of Chinese and American poets and translators that took place a couple of years ago. My encounters with the older Chinese poet took place at that event."

KENNETH KOCH was born in Cincinnati, Ohio, in 1925. He lives in New York City and teaches at Columbia University. His most recent books of poetry are *New Addresses* (2000), *Straits* (1998), *One Train* (1994), and *On *the Great Atlantic Rainway: Selected Poems 1950–1988* (1994), all from Knopf. Also published recently were two books about poetry: *The Art of Poetry* (University of Michigan, 1996) and *Making Your Own Days* (Scribner, 1998). A book of plays, *The Gold Standard,* was published by Knopf in 1996; and an opera for which he wrote the libretto (*The Banquet,* music by Marcello Panni) is being performed in Genoa, Rome, and Florence in 2001.

Of "To World War Two," Koch writes: "I spent about three years in the army during World War Two, some of it in combat in the Philippines. I wrote a few poems about being in the war when I was still a soldier, but hadn't written any since then until the device of talking to World War Two as if it were a person—or at least someone or something that could understand what I said—somehow enabled me to do so. Without this odd device of directly addressing the war I couldn't imagine how to get the right tone in talking about my experience of it. I found I had something to say and was happy to be able to say it. The poem was originally two poems, one 'To the United States Army' and the other 'To World War Two.' Neither by itself got enough of the subject to be quite what I wanted."

NOELLE KOCOT was born on November 14, 1969, in Brooklyn, where she now lives with her husband of eight years, composer/pianist Damon Tomblin. She graduated from Oberlin College and the University of Florida, and works as a training administrator. She has received the S. J. Marks Memorial Award from *The American Poetry Review* (1997) and a fellowship from the National Endowment for the Arts (2001). Her first book of poetry, *4,* was published in May 2001 by Four Way Books. She has no hobbies to speak of.

Of "Consolations Before an Affair, Upper West Side," Kocot writes: "I wrote this poem the morning after the experience in the poem, that is, having dinner on New York's Upper West Side with someone, a married poet, who was contemplating having an affair with another married poet. She asked me what I thought, and I told her that I thought it would only make her unhappy, which it did actually wind up doing.

"The poem is far more narrative and grounded and overtly confessional than most of my work and for that reason alone, it is one of my favorites, it really is the exception that proves the rule. The title is based on a poem that I love by James Tate, 'Consolations After an Affair.' The poem ends a line before I thought it should, but the editors of *Another Chicago Magazine* thought it should go (it is extremely melodramatic: 'Who has faltered, continually, on the upswing') and I thought maybe they were right. In any case, what is, is."

JOHN KOETHE was born on December 25, 1945, in San Diego, and was educated at Princeton and Harvard Universities. He has published five books of poetry, most recently *The Constructor* (HarperCollins, 1999), which was a finalist for the Lenore Marshall Prize and *The New Yorker* Book Award, and *Falling Water* (HarperCollins, 1997), which received the Kingsley Tufts Award. He is also the author of *Poetry at One Remove: Essays* (University of Michigan Press, 2000) and *The Continuity of Wittgenstein's Thought* (Cornell University Press, 1996). He is professor of philosophy at the University of Wisconsin, Milwaukee. "Songs of the Valley" will be included in *North Point North: New and Selected Poems,* to be published by HarperCollins in early 2002.

Of "Songs of the Valley," Koethe writes: "Though Wallace Stevens is one of the principle influences on my work, I almost never set out to write a poem in Stevens's manner (a partial exception is a long poem called 'The Secret Amplitude,' which was included in *The Best American Poetry 1998*). But a few years ago I was reading an article in which Helen Vendler talked about him, and the opening lines of 'Songs of the Valley' popped into my head, and I decided to write a short poem using some of Stevens's rhetoric and his sense of dualities and oppositions. Actually, the opening line is not the one that originally occurred to me, which was 'There are two choirs, one sung in space.' But several people to whom I showed the poem complained that choirs aren't sung, and while the idea still seemed fine to me, I didn't want readers to get hung up on the first line of the poem, so I changed it."

YUSEF KOMUNYAKAA was born in Bogalusa, Louisiana, in 1947. He received the Bronze Star for his service as a correspondent in Vietnam. His most recent books include *Pleasure Dome: New and Collected Poems, 1975–1999* (Wesleyan), *Talking Dirty to the Gods* (poems, Farrar, Straus and Giroux), and *Blue Notes: Essays, Interviews and Commentaries* (Poets on Poetry Series, University of Michigan Press), both in 2000. Among his other titles are *Thieves of Paradise,* a finalist for the 1999 National Book Critics Circle Award, and *Neon Vernacular: New and Selected Poems 1977–1989,* winner of the 1994 Pulitzer Prize in poetry. He wrote the lyrics for *Thirteen Kinds of Desire* (Cornucopia Productions, 2000), sung by jazz singer Pamela Knowles. Elected to the Board of Chancellors of the Academy of American Poets in 1999, he teaches at Princeton University.

Asked about his "relationship to form, particularly the 'sixteen-line approach,'" Komunyakaa replied: "It tells me I can write about anything and basically collapse whatever my observations and meditations are into a structure—if it's on metaphysics, a scientific principle, or the ritual of an insect or an animal—I can collapse it into that sixteen-line structure and, hopefully, through that compression be surprised. I'm saying more than I could say in thirty lines."

MARK LEVINE was born in Flushing, New York, in 1965. He grew up in Toronto and was educated at Brown University and the University of Iowa. He has published two books of poems: *Debt* (William Morrow, 1993) and *Enola Gay* (University of California Press, 2000). He is a member of the permanent faculty of the University of Iowa Writers' Workshop, where he teaches each fall. The rest of the year he lives in Brooklyn and works as a journalist for *The New Yorker* and other magazines.

Levine writes: "In 'Wedding Day,' the last poem in my book *Enola Gay*, some of the images that accumulate over the course of that book— craters, debris, marshes, ships, trumpets, atoms, trains—reappear in a setting that is essentially personal, even, obliquely, autobiographical. To me, it is a poem that tries to think about having 'an appointment with elsewhere,' with the place that is not the altar, not the book of poems one might have just read, not the site from which one is speaking. The desire to be here—the need to be elsewhere—the fact of being unreconciled. And the mislaid plans for a wedding ceremony on the longest day of the year."

SARAH MANGUSO was born in Newton, Massachusetts, in 1974. She received a B.A. from Harvard University and an M.F.A. from the University of Iowa, where she was a Truman Capote Fellow in creative writing. She is the author of *The Captain Lands in Paradise,* forthcoming from Alice James Books, and her poems have appeared in *American Letters & Commentary, The American Poetry Review, The Iowa Review,* and *The New Republic.* She works as a copy editor and book critic and lives in New York City.

Of "The Rider," Manguso writes: "The low prairie in the last line is the low prairie of western South Dakota, a state I drove across in 1999. At the time, it seemed like the end of the world."

J. D MCCLATCHY was born in Bryn Mawr, Pennsylvania, in 1945. He lives in New York City and in Stonington, Connecticut. He is editor of *The Yale Review* and has taught at Yale, Princeton, UCLA, and Columbia. He has written four books of poems: *Scenes from Another Life* (Braziller, 1981), *Stars Principal* (Macmillan, 1986), *The Rest of the Way* (Knopf, 1990), and *Ten Commandments* (Knopf, 1998). Two collections of his essays have appeared: *White Paper* (1989) and *Twenty Questions* (1998), both from Columbia University Press. In addition, he has written four opera libretti and edited many books, including *The Vintage Book of Contemporary American Poetry* (1990) and *The Vintage Book of Contemporary World Poetry* (1996). He is a chancellor of the Academy of American Poets.

Of "Tattoos," McClatchy writes: "Poems in their own way—ornamenting the white page—are tattoos: Their ink at its most precise can draw blood and make a moment endure. We admire tattoos, as we value poems, equally for their respect of convention and their impulse toward innovation. This poem—all in syllabics—is itself a set of patterns, that of its first section mirroring its third in matching anecdotes and scaffolding, and its middle part a discursive run of lines in limping, odd-numbered pairs. With a pointed but, I hope, forgivable swagger, I've used some insider lingo here, from a reference to the Great Lakes Naval Training Center and parlor slang like 'flashes' (predesigned emblems) or 'sleeve' (a tattooed scene that covers one's arm, wrist to shoulder) all the way to the Maori creation myth. The first part tiptoes around what used to be called 'unspoken desires.' The third part plunges into their cosmic depths. The middle part, I trust, turns inside out what the other, more melodramatic sections struggle to conceal. And two footnotes: 1) George Seferis, in his diary: 'In essence, the poet has only one theme: his living body,' and 2) I should add, of course, that I don't myself have a tattoo."

COLLEEN J. MCELROY lives in Seattle, Washington. Her most recently published book of poems is *Travelling Music* (Story Line Press, 1998). Other recent publications include her travel memoirs, *A Long Way from St. Louie* (Coffee House Press, 1997), and a work of creative nonfiction, *Over the Lip of the World: Among the Storytellers of Madagascar* (University of Washington Press, 1999). She has received a Before Columbus American Book Award. McElroy is editor in chief of the *Seattle Review* and teaches at the University of Washington in Seattle. She is currently working on a novel, teaching, and planning her next journey to some far-flung corner of the globe that will force her travel agent to pull out yet another map.

Of "Mae West Chats It Up with Bessie Smith," McElroy writes: "I could start with my grandmother's attic and the years during World War II when I was an only child dancing to tunes on the Victrola. I loved the ladies of torch songs and blues, so Bessie and Mae have been in my head for years. The poem is out of a collection of love poems, my second such collection. As with my first collection, I am the skeptic who doesn't 'know what love is' but has much to say about its regrets. What better voices than the seasoned comments of experience, like Mae West and Bessie Smith, *les femmes d'un certain âge,* living a little dangerously, always outrageous, outspoken, and out to get the most from life. They are my heroes, and more often than not, speak to me when I've once again ventured into that place where my heart beats too loudly. But most of all, they give me wit in those times when I could be flattened by the Blues. It took me half a century to get here, but I can't say it's been boring."

HEATHER MCHUGH was born in California in 1948. She is a professor of poetry at the University of Washington in Seattle; she frequently teaches in the low-residency MFA program at Warren Wilson College. Her most recent books are *The Father of the Predicaments* (poems, Wesleyan University Press/University Press of New England, 1999); *Broken English: Poetry and Partiality* (literary essays, Wesleyan University Press, rpt. 1999); and a cotranslation with her husband, Nikolai Popov, of *Glottal Stop: 101 Poems by Paul Celan* (Wesleyan University Press, 2000).

Of "My One," McHugh writes: "The poem proceeds from an anagrammatical insight into the relation between love and possessiveness. I'm not sure whether *homo* or *sui* is the generis of *cide* (some things a poet must not decide); but the poem's ecstatic coinages are, I trust, sufficiently ironized to take some of the shine off the romantic occasion. The old yearning of lovers to ask 'How much?' is as ruinous as it is revealing."

HARRYETTE MULLEN was born in Florence, Alabama, birthplace of blues man W. C. Handy, and grew up in Fort Worth, Texas, home of jazz leader Ornette Coleman. Mullen teaches English and African American Studies at UCLA. She is the author of five books of poetry: *Tree Tall Woman* (Energy Earth Communications, 1981), *Trimmings* (Tender Buttons Books, 1991), *S*PeRM**K*T* (Singing Horse Press, 1992), *Muse & Drudge* (Singing Horse Press, 1995), and *Sleeping with the Dictionary* (University of California Press, 2001). Parts of *Muse & Drudge* have been set to music in T. J. Anderson's *Seven Cabaret Songs* and Christine

Baczewska's *O Rose.* "Music for Homemade Instruments" is included in *Sleeping with the Dictionary.*

Of "Music for Homemade Instruments," Mullen writes: "A few years ago, I had the pleasure of performing with Douglas Ewart at Woodland Pattern Book Center in Milwaukee. Imagining a program divided between his music and my poetry, I looked forward to meeting this acclaimed jazz musician, who plays and creates many instruments, including bamboo flutes and didgeridoos. However, I was startled when our hosts suggested that we try a spontaneous collaboration before a live audience. Our performance was also to be recorded for a local radio broadcast. Douglas Ewart is a master of improvisation, but I was out of my depth. Usually, I just read the poetry. This was my first experience attempting a verbal-musical duet with an instrumentalist, but I survived that baptism, thanks to Doug's reassuring presence, expertise, and grace. The title of my poem is borrowed from Music for Homemade Instruments, an ensemble of classically trained musicians who invent, build, compose for, perform on, and teach with musical instruments built from found objects. This prose poem of recycled language, my tribute to Douglas, is a playful transformation of words into other words, as the jazz player improvises with musical notes and the jazz vocalist doodles with nonsense syllables."

CAROL MUSKE DUKES was born on December 17, 1945, in St. Paul, Minnesota. She directs the graduate program in creative writing at the University of Southern California. She is the author of six books of poems, most recently, *An Octave Above Thunder* (Penguin, 1997); three novels, most recently, *Life After Death* (Random House, 2001); and two books of criticism: *Women and Poetry* (University of Michigan Press, 1997) and the forthcoming *A Poet in Hollywood* (Random House, 2002).

Muske Dukes writes: " 'Our Kitty' is my way of imagining the return of John Keats—in the persona of a showgirl named Kitty. The 'untaken hand' turns up in a poem fragment by Keats, and seems to me to represent the proffered hand of Poetry itself."

ALICE NOTLEY was born in Bisbee, Arizona, on November 8, 1945, and grew up in Needles, California. She was educated at Barnard College and the University of Iowa Writers' Workshop. She lived a peripatetic poet's life until settling in New York's Lower East Side for sixteen years beginning in the early 1970s. Her book-length poem *The Descent of Alette* was published by Penguin in 1996. Her last book, *Mysteries of Small Houses*

(Penguin, 1998), was a finalist for the Pulitzer Prize and won the *Los Angeles Times* Book Award for Poetry. A book-length poem, *Disobedience,* is forthcoming from Penguin in the fall of 2001. Notley lives in Paris, where she teaches creative writing at the British Institute.

Notley writes: " 'Where Leftover Misery Goes' is from a very long manuscript (over three hundred pages) entitled *Reason and Other Women.* The book is intended to show the author herself in the process of thought; thus typos and mistakes are left in as standing for 'mind fuzz,' and repetition both maintains momentum and indicates stasis, in the way the two combine in thinking. However the book is also tied in with the concept of a Byzantine Church with all its icons and mosaics: permanent images or stories one never shakes, also the little dots or pieces of thinking, also the sacrality of consciousness. This particular poem dwells on events and dreams that occurred fifteen years before the writing of the poem but can never be lost: they are unpleasant but iconic. They have perhaps become beautiful."

SHARON OLDS was born in San Francisco in 1942. She teaches at New York University and lives in New York City. Her most recent books are *The Wellspring* (1996) and *Blood, Tin, Straw* (1999), both from Knopf.

Of "His Costume," Olds writes: "When I stop a moment and look at a poem of mine, not to rewrite it but to try to see it, it's the texture—the rhyme and beat—that come forward for me: the four-beat lines, and the sounds the strong accents fall on. And I see how this poem, when it gets its run on, is really more two-beat: so the sort of hearts or cores of it (as in geologic sea-floor readings) for me are

> dress . . . . . tennis
> breasts . . . breasts
> blonde . . . . lip
> body . . . . . . grace

and

> skirt . . . . . book
> nurse . . . . . drink
> round . . . . . care (ma*sc*ara)
> salt . . . . . . mother

—lots of liquidness, drooling, lipping, nourishing. (By 'core' I guess I mean structural beam-work of music, and density of image—form:content::costume:core.) (A poem *is* its music, that's the main thing.)"

KATHLEEN OSSIP was born in Albany, New York, in 1959. She received an M.F.A. from the New School University, where she now teaches a poetry workshop. Her poems have appeared in *The Antioch Review, American Letters & Commentary, The Journal,* and *Barrow Street.* She works as a writer of educational materials and lives with her husband and daughter in Westchester County, New York.

Of "The Nature of Things," Ossip writes: "One of the many pleasures of working with Susan Wheeler was the opportunity to peer at the Robert Lostutter painting that hung in the hallway of her apartment. The painting showed a man morphing into an exotic bird—the artist's constant subject. To my eye, the man looked slightly tormented and utterly quotidian.

"I wanted to create a narrative frame for the picture and I wanted to talk soothingly to the man. From those impulses came my first-and-only ekphrastic poem. (In some of Lostutter's paintings, there are two figures: thus the pal.)"

GRACE PALEY was born in the Bronx in 1922 to Russian Jewish immigrants. She has two grown children and three grandchildren and is now married to Robert Nichols—Russian, Yiddish, and English are all spoken in her home. She went to Hunter College and New York University; she finished neither. After spending most of her life in New York, she moved to Vermont fifteen years ago; she loves both places and continues to visit New York frequently. Her books of stories include *The Little Disturbances of Man* (1959), *Enormous Changes at the Last Minute* (1974), *Later the Same Day* (Penguin, 1986), *Long Walks and Intimate Talks* (Feminist Press, 1991), *The Collected Stories* (Farrar, Straus and Giroux, 1994), and *Just as I Thought* (Farrar, Straus and Giroux, 1998). Her books of poems include *New and Collected Poems* (Tilbury Press, 1992) and *Begin Again: Collected Poems* (Farrar, Straus and Giroux, 2001).

Of "Here," Paley writes: "I have always been a political person and have described myself as a combative pacifist and cooperative anarchist. The poem, I guess, is a love poem to my old man, who is as interested in this harsh world as I and even more eager to change it. We are both old and hate to leave the world even worse than we found it."

MICHAEL PALMER was born in New York City in 1943 and has lived in San Francisco since 1969. He has published nine collections of poetry and taught at many universities. He has worked extensively with contemporary dance for twenty-five years and has collaborated with numerous visual artists and composers. His most recent collections are *At Passages* (New Directions, 1995), *The Lion Bridge (Selected Poems 1972–1995)* (New Directions, 1998), and *The Promises of Glass* (New Directions, 2000). A prose work, *The Danish Notebook,* was published by Avec Books in 1999. With Régis Bonvicino and Nelson Ascher, he edited and helped to translate *Nothing the Sun Could Not Explain: 20 Contemporary Brazilian Poets* (Sun & Moon Press, 1997). Among his other translations are *Theory of Tables* by Emmanuel Hocquard (o-blek editions, 1992) and Alexei Parshchikov's *Blue Vitriol* (Avec Press, 1994). His own writings have been translated into more than twenty languages.

Of "Untitled (February 2000)," Palmer writes: "Not much I would wish to add to what is there / not there, visible / not visible in the poem. A chance encounter ('objective chance'?) with an air of unreality about it. Composed over a couple of weeks, the final chance element being its completion on Leap Year Day. This fact, as it suddenly dawned on me, seemed to confirm the out-of-time character of the entire experience. The poem goes out for a walk. What does it see and hear, and when, and who is to say?"

JOHN PECK was born in Pittsburgh, Pennsylvania, in 1941, and is now divorced, with one daughter, Ingrid. Currently he works as a freelance and contract editor, a Jungian analyst, and occasionally as an adjunct professor. A professional reshuffle at mid-career took him to Switzerland, where he worked for eight years as an editor, professor, and jack-of-all-trades while training in Jung's complex psychology (to use his own name for it). His eight books include *Shagbark* (Bobbs-Merrill, 1972), *The Broken Blockhouse Wall* (Godine, 1978, and Carcanet, 1979), *Poems and Translations of Hi-Lo* (Carcanet, 1991, and Sheep Meadow, 1993), *Argura* (Carcanet, 1993), *Selva Morale* (Carcanet, 1995), *Orestes* (Euripides: Oxford, 1995, with Frank Nisetich), *M and Other Poems* (Northwestern, 1996), and *Collected Shorter Poems 1966–1996* (Carcanet, 1999). An interview with Clive Wilmer appears in *Poets Talking* (Carcanet, 1994). For six of the past eight years he has worked in private practice in southern Vermont.

Of "A Metal Denser Than, and Liquid," Peck writes: "Albert Speer had fascinated me long before Gitta Sereny published her exhaustive portrait of the man, but only on happening to peer again through her microscope (at a public-library book sale) did the fascination recolonize its uncomfortable virus in me. This poem is my homemade antibiotic. While its task is a venerable one—the *examen de conscience*—its very gradual entrance into that task was my experiment. In the course of writing I discovered that the saving prompting which spoke to me—*discernment is not judgment*—I had heard at least five times over the course of several decades: from an Anglican priest, a former Catholic priest turned analyst, two teachers of Theravada meditation, and my fellow poet Teresa Iverson. So I am happy to acknowledge this small band of furtherers in the art of right-targeting. Their point not only helped me in my minor wrestle with a mightily destructive *artiste manqué,* whose only valid work, he said, was his design for a street lamp in Berlin. It also offers help, I would surmise, to any artist or museum-quality liberal who admires the work of W. B. Yeats, Djuna Barnes, or Marguerite Yourcenar while acknowledging the discomfiting engagement of their sensibilities with themes and atmospheres (or with the spiritual entrails, perhaps?) of what collectively we call 'fascism.' We are not yet able to handle such terms cleanly, and I suspect that we shall succeed in doing so only once we are able to face, while pointing the finger at others, our own mirrors."

LUCIA PERILLO was born in 1958 and grew up in the suburbs of New York City. Her latest book of poems is *The Oldest Map with the Name America* (Random House, 1999). She has taught at Southern Illinois University and now lives in Washington State.

Of "The Ghost Shirt," Perillo writes: The ghost shirt—that which we naively believe protects us—was something that I had often used naively as a poetic trope. I finally stumbled on a real one in the Museum of Natural History in New York while on a trip back east, where I was camping for a few days on various friends' couches, estranged from my usual encounters with newspapers and TV. As I made my way home to my parents' house in the suburbs, I found myself engulfed in a day-of-the-locust style human crush, and it was only as I waited on the train that I learned what was happening: the officers who'd assaulted Rodney King had been acquitted, and the city was emptying out. It was one of the few times in my life that I've truly felt swept up in capital-H History.

"I wrote the poem a few years later while studying Dante's *Inferno* under the tutelage of Dr. Edward Brunner at Southern Illinois University, and that was what impelled me to use the terza rima form to describe what was partly an underground experience. I should also say that a Native American woman has chastised me for using the word Sioux instead of the more accurate Lakota, and for my contention that belief in the ghost shirt was naive. Perhaps I merely cannot understand the mechanism of its effect."

CARL PHILLIPS was born in Everett, Washington, in 1959. He i
author of five books of poetry: *The Tether* (Farrar, Straus and Gi
2001), *Pastoral* (Graywolf, 2000), *From the Devotions* (Graywolf, 1
Cortège (Graywolf, 1995), and *In the Blood* (Northeastern, 1992). A recip-
ient of the Morse Prize and awards and fellowships from the Guggen-
heim Foundation, the Academy of American Poets, and the Library of
Congress, he teaches at Washington University, St. Louis.

Of "The Clearing," Phillips writes: "At one point in Homer's *Iliad,* the
Greek general Agamemnon is given instruction by the gods in a dream.
He trusts the dream, he believes the gods. The result is disaster, for the
gods have deliberately given Agamemnon a false dream, in order to tip
the scales in favor of the Trojan army.

"*The Iliad* wasn't on my mind while writing, but the concerns that
arise from that incident are the concerns of my poem: the capacity for
deception in what we trust most, be it a deity, a lover, or (more distress-
ing) the self; the distance that—swiftly, subtly—can come to exist
between our actual selves and those that we construct, either out of a
longing not to see the truth of ourselves or from an inability to do so; and
that space in which to know what is 'wrong' is not necessarily to under-
stand what is 'right,' even as understanding is rarely the same as doing,
or so I have found.

"Another way to put it: not knowing where to turn, instead I built
myself a wall against what I would and would not turn from. The
poem is the result."

ROBERT PINSKY was born in Long Branch, New Jersey, in 1940. He
served three terms as Poet Laureate of the United States. His most
recent book of poems, *Jersey Rain,* was published by Farrar, Straus and
Giroux in 2000. He has translated Dante's *Inferno.* He teaches at Boston
University and is coeditor of *Americans' Favorite Poems,* an anthology of
poems introduced by readers who selected them, published by Norton
in 1999.

Of "Jersey Rain," Pinsky writes: "The past has certain resemblances
to rain. Rain is a source of life, a fundamental replenisher. It makes
things grow. It transforms our vision, making things we look at blurrier
or sharper, less visible or more stark. It can be beautiful.

"And it can ruin a weekend. It can be depressing. It can make us feel
confined.

"My poem is a pretty straightforward account of these similarities
between rain and the past. And for me, the rain is in some ways always

a New Jersey rain, just as the past is most certainly first of all a New Jersey past."

CLAUDIA RANKINE was born in Kingston, Jamaica, in 1963, and now lives in New York City. She is the author of three volumes of poetry, most recently *PLOT* (Grove Press, 2001). Her earlier books were *Nothing in Nature Is Private* (Cleveland State, 1994) and *The End of the Alphabet* (Grove Press, 1998). She has coedited with Juliana Spahr a collection of essays entitled *American Women Poets in the 21st Century,* which will be published by Wesleyan University Press in fall 2001. The collection includes essays by and about Rae Armantrout, Mei-mei Berssenbrugge, Lucie Brock-Broido, Jorie Graham, Barbara Guest, Lyn Hejinian, Brenda Hillman, Susan Howe, Ann Lauterbach, and Harryette Mullen. She teaches at Barnard College, and is the director of Women Poets at Barnard.

Rankine writes: "Katie Couric of the *Today* show on NBC interviewed a doctor who argued that women were intended to have children and that, because more and more women were choosing not to have them, all kinds of things were going awry in their bodies. He contended that a childless woman should stay on birth control pills all the time, including the week she normally bleeds. I forget now what this was supposed to achieve. Another doctor—Doctor Love from Santa Cruz perhaps, beamed into the studio via satellite—was outraged. This five-minute interview remained with me in the form of a warning to those women and had something to do with my writing 'A short narrative of breasts and wombs.' "

ADRIENNE RICH was born in Baltimore, Maryland, in 1929. She graduated from Radcliffe College in 1951, the year her first book, *A Change of World,* was chosen by W. H. Auden for the Yale Series of Younger Poets. She has published fifteen books of poetry and five of prose, including *Blood, Bread and Poetry* (Norton, 1986), *What Is Found There: Notebooks on Poetry and Politics* (Norton, 1993), and *Arts of the Possible: Essays and Conversations* (Norton, 2001). "Architect" appears in her most recent book of poems, *Fox* (Norton, 2001). For the past fifteen years she has lived in California. She was guest editor of *The Best American Poetry 1996.*

Of "Architect," Rich writes: "Let's say this architect was going through a bad, a degraded period. His work depends on popularity and nostalgia and the dictates of wealth; more literally, on the physical labor of others. He had done better in the past and perhaps his future work will redeem this shoddy interval. To what extent is his work determined by his time, to what extent does he collaborate? For better or for worse, architecture is the most social of the arts, most reflective of power and money relationships. Many of the other poems in *Fox* allude to art's stubborn transfusions of hope and energy, even in periods of social disintegration."

JAMES RICHARDSON was born in Bradenton, Florida, in 1950, and grew up in Garden City, New York. He is professor of creative writing and English at Princeton University, where he has taught since 1980. His collections of poems include *Reservations* (Princeton University Press, 1977); *Second Guesses* (Wesleyan University Press, 1984); *As If* (Persea Books, 1992), which was selected by Amy Clampitt for the National Poetry Series; *A Suite for Lucretians* (Quarterly Review of Literature Poetry Series, 1999); and *How Things Are* (Carnegie Mellon University Press, 2000). He has also written two critical studies, *Thomas Hardy: The Poetry of Necessity* (University of Chicago Press, 1977) and *Vanishing Lives: Tennyson, Rossetti, Swinburne, and Yeats* (University Press of Virginia, 1988).

Of "Vectors: Forty-five Aphorisms and Ten-second Essays," Richardson writes: "Back in 1993, I was looking at Montaigne for an essay to be called 'On Likeness.' A note sent me to the maxims of La Rochefoucauld, which I read not only with delight, but with eager disagreement. 'Wait, that's not right,' I'd mutter, or 'That's not *all*,' scribbling some correction or rotation of one of his insights. Soon, aphorisms were fizzing up in response to whatever I was reading—which was, more and more, Antonio Porchia, Marie von Ebner-Eschenbach, and *The Oxford Book of Aphorisms*—and I hardly had the attention span for longer thought. This was a distracting, obviously useless, and vaguely guilty pleasure, like playing video games or eating corn chips. Who'd want to hear my strictures and paradoxes? What about 'Show, don't tell'? What about 'negative capability'? If they mean anything, I suppose, they mean a writer had better be content not knowing exactly what he's doing, and I certainly didn't. And, after all, the best time is stolen time. Though I sometimes struggled heroically not to write it, *Vectors: Five Hundred Aphorisms and Ten-second Essays* will be published by Chase Twichell's new Ausable Press in fall 2001. As for that essay, it's . . . in progress."

RACHEL ROSE is a dual Canadian/American citizen who was born in Vancouver, Canada, in 1970. She has lived on Hornby Island in Canada, Fidalgo Island in Washington State, as well as in Seattle, Vancouver,

Montreal, and Maebashi, Japan, and is both drawn to and repelled by the intricacies of island life. She is currently a housewife and stay-at-home mother in Vancouver, where she lives with her partner, Isabelle, and son, Benjamin. Her first book of poetry is *Giving My Body To Science* (McGill/Queen's University Press), which was a finalist for the Gerald Lampert Award, the Pat Lowther Award, the Grand Prix du Livre de Montréal, and which won the Quebec Writer's Federation Poetry Award for 2000.

Rose writes: "Like any good foreigner living in another country, while I lived in Japan I read as much as I could about Japanese culture and traditions, both in books written by other foreigners and books written by the Japanese themselves for the purpose of educating visitors. The contradictions in these books were intriguing enough, but then, as the only American representative to which they had access, I was expected to answer all the questions my Japanese students posed: Why were we Americans so dangerously armed? Why couldn't we stay married?

"I went to Japan just after graduating from university, with the unspoken assumption that North America, despite its faults, was the most advanced area in the world. From the moment of my arrival, I was challenged by the steadfast belief of most Japanese that Japan was, despite its faults, superior to any country on earth. It was from these challenges and contradictions that these poems emerged, as I wrestled with the very concept of anthropology."

MARY RUEFLE was born in McKeesport, Pennsylvania, in 1952. She has received a National Endowment for the Arts Fellowship, a Whiting Writer's Award, and an award in literature from the American Academy of Arts and Letters. Her publications include five books of poems: *Memling's Veil* (University of Alabama Press, 1982), *Life Without Speaking* (University of Alabama Press, 1987), *The Adamant* (University of Iowa Press, 1989), *Cold Pluto* (Carnegie Mellon University Press, 1996), and *Post Meridian* (Carnegie Mellon University Press, 2000). She lives in Massachusetts and teaches in the MFA writing program at Vermont College. Her work appeared in *The Best American Poetry 1997*.

Of "Furtherness," Ruefle writes: "I look at this poem and I don't know what to say: when was it written, and where? I know the opening stanza is a description of the funeral of William Morris, and the sixth a description of Emily Dickinson's. The others—made up—though the third could be Stalin or Snow White, couldn't it? I always wanted to write a poem with the word *excelsis* in it—funny that it wound up in a poem with so many deaths. Ordure—what does that mean? My mother had a stainless steel coffin covered with photographs, but she died after the poem was written—would I add that now? No, I would add a stainless steel coffin covered with the flag of an obscure nation: so it goes. Poetry is murderous and off-kilter in all the ways those pies are, there at the end—all the while necessary and good—whatever it takes to sustain life, which will always go on its way."

JAMES SCHUYLER was born in Chicago in 1923. *Freely Espousing,* his first collection of poems, did not appear until he was forty-six. His subsequent books include *The Crystal Lithium* (1972), *Hymn to Life* (Random House, 1974), *The Morning of the Poem* (Farrar, Straus and Giroux, 1980), *A Few Days* (Random House, 1985), and the posthumous *Collected Poems* (Farrar, Straus and Giroux, 1993). *The Morning of the Poem* won the Pulitzer Prize. He was also the author of three novels, one of them, *A Nest of Ninnies,* written in collaboration with John Ashbery. Schuyler died in New York City in April 1991. *The Diary of James Schuyler,* edited by Nathan Kernan, was published in 1997, and Schuyler's *Selected Art Writings,* edited by Simon Pettet, in 1998, both from Black Sparrow Press. A paperback edition of *Alfred and Guinevere* (1958), Schuyler's first novel, is newly available from The New York Review of Books. Douglas Crase has written that he regarded Schuyler as his "moralist of the everyday": "The exciting thing about knowing as well as reading Jimmy was to observe how his ethics seemed to emerge directly from the life around us. . . . One evening after dinner at our apartment he was admiring the pink cover Robert Dash had done for John Koethe's book *The Late Wisconsin Spring.* It was, he said, 'a very fine pink.' But Jimmy, I warned, Bob says it's the wrong pink. Jimmy regarded me silently for a moment, then in that voice of sudden gravity he said, 'Only if you had another pink in mind.'"

"Along Overgrown Paths" was discovered in the John Ashbery archive of the Houghton Library at Harvard University. It had been lost twice. Schuyler sent a typed copy of the poem, dated April 23, 1968, to Ashbery in a letter four years later. "The other day I moved my filing cabinet and under it was this poem," Schuyler explained. "It's nothing much, but it does memorialize a notable trip to Pultneyville" (the upstate New York town where Ashbery's mother then lived). Librarians may have found the letter and its contents difficult to file; the letter is addressed to "Lotta Crust" from "Miss American Pie," though it is signed "Jimmy" and the initials "JS" appear beside the date on the typescript of the poem.

CHARLES SIMIC was born in Belgrade, Yugoslavia, in 1938, and immigrated to the United States in 1954. As a poet and translator, he has published more than sixty books in this country and abroad since 1967. He teaches American literature and creative writing at the University of New Hampshire. Among his numerous awards are the MacArthur Fellowship and the Pulitzer Prize. *Jackstraws,* a new book of poems, and *Selected Early Poems* were published by Harcourt Brace in 1999. He writes criticism regularly for *The New York Review of Books.* His book of memoirs, *A Fly in the Soup,* appeared from the University of Michigan Press in 2000. He was the guest editor of *The Best American Poetry 1992.*

Of "Night Picnic," Simic writes: "Before one thinks or says anything, I suppose, one ought to look at the sky at night first. For almost thirty years I have lived in the country surrounded by miles of woods. In the summer we usually dine outdoors or just sit late past bedtime, talking and sipping wine in the dark. The poem comes out of the memory of many such nights."

LARISSA SZPORLUK was born in Ann Arbor, Michigan, in 1967. She is the mother of two young children and lives with her husband, Carlo Celli, in Bowling Green, Ohio, where she sometimes teaches creative writing at Bowling Green State University. She is the author of *Dark Sky Question* (Beacon Press, 1998) and *Isolato* (University of Iowa Press, 2000), and has just completed her third manuscript, *The Wind, Master Cherry, The Wind.*

Szporluk writes: " 'Meteor' is unusually frank. It felt good to write. The metaphor came easily. There is a tremendous need, after bearing children, to be wickedly selfish and perhaps that's why even 'Nero' entered the poem naturally. Because the poem was guided by fury rather than the more typical patching and plodding, I am refreshingly detached from any artistic concerns—I wouldn't change a thing."

SUSAN STEWART was born in York, Pennsylvania, in 1952, and is the author of three books of poems, most recently *The Forest* from the University of Chicago Press. She teaches at the University of Pennsylvania and in 2000 delivered the Beckman lectures at the University of California at Berkeley. Her four books of criticism include *On Longing* and the forthcoming *Poetry and the Fate of the Senses,* and she often writes on contemporary art. Her translation with Brunella Antomarini of the poems of the Scuola Romana painter Scipione will appear from Charta in Milan in the coming year, as well as a translation with Wesley Smith of Euripides' *Andromache* in the new Oxford series of classical tragedies.

Stewart writes: " 'Apple' is the 'A' in an alphabet of georgics and their shadows that makes up my next book of poems. The georgics are poems of instruction from one generation to another and in writing 'Apple' I talked with everyone I knew about memories of, and names for, and advice about growing, apples. The poem is an archive of the voices of others, including by now the voices of the dead."

JAMES TATE was born in Kansas City, Missouri, in 1943. His most recent book of poems, *Memoir of the Hawk,* was published by Ecco/Harper-Collins in 2001. He is the author of fourteen previous books of poetry, among them *Shroud of the Gnome* (Ecco, 1997), *Worshipful Company of Fletchers* (Ecco, 1994), and *Selected Poems* (Wesleyan University Press, 1991). He has won the Pulitzer Prize and the National Book Award. He teaches at the University of Massachusetts in Amherst and was the guest editor of *The Best American Poetry 1997*.

Asked about his prose poems, Tate once replied, "The only thing that matters in a prose poem is the absolute quickness of telling this contained story. It's anecdotal, very brief, and to the point. There's no reason to break off those lines and call it verse."

BERNARD WELT was born in Houston, Texas, in 1952, and grew up in Arlington, Virginia. He received an M.A. in writing from the Johns Hopkins University and a Ph.D. in literary studies from the American University. As a professor of academic studies at the Corcoran College of Art and Design in Washington, DC, he teaches courses in cinema and interdisciplinary humanities studies. His essays for the Los Angeles journal *Art issues* were collected in *Mythomania: Fantasies, Fables, and Sheer Lies in Contemporary American Popular Art* (Art issues Press, 1996). In 1992, he was a one-show champion on the television game show *Jeopardy!,* a twenty-two-minute effort that garnered more attention than any writing he has ever done. He is the author of one book of poems, *Serenade* (Z Press, 1979).

Welt writes: " 'I stopped writing poetry . . .' almost didn't get written, because—well, *I'd stopped writing poetry.* Most of the testimony, explanations, and excuses offered in the poem are honest, or sincere, or authentic, or whatever you are left having to call it when you are genuinely trying to account to yourself for your own behavior. As a lot of your better poets, from Catullus to Joe Brainard, must have discovered, the first person enforces a strange duality, opening up the floodgates of real emotion and memory while leaving you in the uncomfortable position of experiencing yourself as a literary character. That discomfort is the main thing I think of when people speak of a poet's *voice*.

"When I saw Judith Hall of the *Antioch Review* at the St. Mary's Poetry Festival in Maryland and she encouraged me to contribute to a special issue on poetry in the year 2000, I was not only very grateful but happy, because I discovered that my ideas for an essay worked better as a sort of self-consuming poem (which Judith then had to talk me into actually writing). I blurted out on the page whatever half-baked idea popped into my head, then I'd get interested in why it came out in those words rather than any others. If I were writing an essay I'd stop at that point and remind myself that I'm more concerned with developing my ideas than obsessing about the aroma of words and phrases. But in writing a poem I surrender to my fascination with the *totality* of the powers of words, not just their denotative faculty; I'm thinking of how language works rather than what I want from it (which always misleads me). And then I really do fall in love with the stanza all over again, and enjambment, and internal rhyme, and I can imitate other writers' styles intentionally and ironically instead of just stealing from them, and I get to feeling that the strange hesitation I often display at line breaks isn't only a tic (though it is) but something I actually have to say."

DEAN YOUNG was born in Columbia, Pennsylvania, in 1955. He has received a fellowship from the Fine Arts Work Center in Provincetown, a Wallace Stegner fellowship from Stanford University, and two fellowships from the National Endowment for the Arts. He has published four books of poems including *Strike Anywhere,* which won the Colorado Poetry Prize, and *First Course in Turbulence* (University of Pittsburgh Press, 1999).

Of "Sources of the Delaware," Young writes: "First off, I have to note that I wrote this poem before the story broke about our President Clinton's oral activities in the oval office. I was trying to get a bunch of rather disparate material to fly in some kind of formation, weird art-world events, pseudo-myth, something I'd written about a phone conversation with a friend. What seemed to be wanted to hold this stuff together for me on the page was a sense of current, of unavoidable and unopposable forward flood. So of course it turned into a love poem."

RACHEL ZUCKER was born in New York City in 1971. She grew up in Greenwich Village, the only child of a storyteller/writer and a gem dealer/writer, and was educated at Yale and the Iowa Writers' Workshop. After working as a photographer, day care teacher, and gem dealer, she taught composition at NYU and poetry at Yale as an adjunct professor. Her poems have appeared in various journals such as *American Poetry Review, Colorado Review, Epoch, Iowa Review,* and *Pleiades.* She publishes *Boomerang! A Contributors' Journal,* now in its tenth issue. She lives in Manhattan with her husband and two young sons.

Zucker writes: "I wrote the first draft of 'In Your Version of Heaven I Am Younger' in September 1998. It was just after the crash of Swiss Air Flight 111 off the shore of Peggy's Cove, Nova Scotia, in which all 229 people aboard died. News of the crash upset me. I remember being particularly disturbed by a report that many of the bodies recovered were wearing life jackets. I became obsessed with imagining the twenty or so minutes during which the passengers knew it was likely that the plane was going to crash. In those same weeks, my husband and I started trying to conceive our first child. Somehow the intersection of these two events—imagining myself full of life, imagining myself about to die—as well as an annoying but typical comment my otherwise endearing husband made ('sometimes I wish you were exactly like you except blond and perky') caused the poem to spark into being. Thinking about it now, I suspect that the language and form of the poem were influenced by the clinical, declarative style of the newspaper articles about the crash."

MAGAZINES WHERE THE POEMS
WERE FIRST PUBLISHED

AGNI, ed. Askold Melnyczuk. Boston University, 236 Bay State Rd., Boston, Massachusetts 02215.

American Letters & Commentary, ed. Anna Rabinowitz. 850 Park Avenue, Suite 5B, New York, New York 10021.

American Poetry Review, eds. Stephen Berg, David Bonanno, and Arthur Vogelsgang. 1721 Walnut Street, Philadelphia, Pennsylvania 19103.

Another Chicago Magazine, eds. Lee Webster and Barry Silesky. 3709 N. Kenmore, Chicago, Illinois 60613.

The Antioch Review, poetry ed. Judith Hall. P. O. Box 148, Yellow Springs, Ohio 45387.

The Atlantic Monthly, poetry ed. Peter Davison. 77 North Washington St., Boston, Massachusetts 02114.

Barrow Street, eds. Patricia Carlin, Peter Covino, Lois Hirschkowitz, and Melissa Hotchkiss. P. O. Box 2017, Old Chelsea Station, New York, New York 10113.

Boston Book Review, ed. Theoharis Constantine Theoharis. 30 Brattle Street, Cambridge, Massachusetts 02138-0372.

Boston Review, poetry eds. Mary Jo Bang and Timothy Donnelly. E53-407, MIT, 30 Wadsworth Street, Cambridge, Massachusetts 02139-4307.

Callaloo, ed. Charles H. Rowell. Dept. of English, 322 Bryan Hall, University of Virginia, Charlottesville, Virginia 22903.

Chain, eds. Jena Osman and Juliana Spahr. Dept. of English, 1733 Donaghho Road, University of Hawai'i. Manoa, Honolulu, Hawaii 96822.

Colorado Review, poetry eds. Jorie Graham and Donald Revell. Dept. of English, Colorado State University, Ft. Collins, Colorado 80523.

Conjunctions, ed. Bradford Morrow. Bard College, Annandale-on-Hudson, New York 12504.

Crab Orchard Review, poetry ed. Allison Joseph. English Dept., Faner Hall, Southern Illinois University, Carbondale, Illinois 62901-4503.

Evansville Review, ed. Dan Walker. 1800 Lincoln Ave., Evansville, Indiana 47722.

Facture, eds. Lindsay Hill and Paul Naylor. P. O. Box 337, Cedar Ridge, California 95924.

Faucheuse, Oakland, California.

Fence, poetry eds. Caroline Crumpacker and Matthew Rohrer. 14 Fifth Avenue, #1A, New York, New York 10011.

Harper's, ed. Lewis H. Lapham. 666 Broadway, New York, New York 10012.

Jubilat, eds. Robert N. Casper, Christian Hawkey, Kelly LeFave, and Michael

Teig. Dept. of English, 482 Bartlett Hall, University of Massachusetts, Amherst, Massachusetts 01003-0510.

The Journal, eds. Kathy Fagan and Michelle Herman. Dept. of English, Ohio State University, 164 W. 17th Ave., Columbus, Ohio 43210.

The Kenyon Review, ed. David Lynn. Kenyon College, Gambier, Ohio 43022.

LIT, editors at large Mark Bibbins, Liz Brown, and Rebecca Reilly. New School University, Writing Program, 66 W. 12th St., #508, New York, New York 10011.

Massachusetts Review, poetry eds. Martín Espada, Anne Halley, and Paul Jenkins. South College, University of Massachusetts, Amherst, Massachusetts 01003.

McSweeney's, ed. Dave Eggers. 394A Ninth Street, Brooklyn, New York 11215.

The Nation, poetry ed. Grace Schulman. 72 Fifth Ave., New York, New York 10011.

The Nebraska Review, poetry ed. Susan Aizenberg. Creative Writing Program, University of Nebraska, Omaha, Nebraska 68182-0324.

New American Writing, eds. Paul Hoover and Maxine Chernoff. 369 Molino Avenue, Mill Valley, California 94941.

The New Republic, poetry ed. Charles Wright. 1220 19th Street NW, Washington, DC 20036.

The New York Review of Books, eds. Barbara Epstein and Robert Silvers. 1755 Broadway, 5th Floor, New York, New York 10019-3780.

The New Yorker, poetry ed. Alice Quinn. 4 Times Square, New York, New York 10036.

Northwest Review, ed. John Witte. 369 PLC, University of Oregon, Eugene, Oregon 97403.

The Paris Review, poetry ed. Richard Howard. 541 E. 72nd St., New York, New York 10021.

Pequod, ed. Mark Rudman. Department of English, New York University, 19 University Place, Room 200, New York, New York 10003.

Ploughshares, eds. Don Lee and David Daniel. Emerson College, 100 Beacon St., Boston, Massachusetts 02116.

Poetry, ed. Joseph Parisi. 60 W. Walton St., Chicago, Illinois 60610-3380.

Quarter After Eight, eds. Tom Noyes, Imad Rahman, and Andrew Touhy. Ellis Hall, Ohio University, Athens, Ohio 45701.

Seneca Review, ed. Deborah Tall. Hobart and William Smith Colleges, Geneva, New York 14456-3397.

Southern Review, poetry eds. James Olney and Dave Smith. 43 Allen Hall, Louisiana State University, Baton Rouge, Louisiana 70803-5005.

Southwest Review, ed. Willard Spiegelman. 307 Fondren Library West, P. O. Box 750374, Southern Methodist University, Dallas, Texas 75275-0374.

The Texas Review, ed. Paul Ruffin. Sam Houston State University, Dept. of English and Foreign Languages, Huntsville, Texas 77341-2146.

Threepenny Review, poetry ed. Wendy Lesser. P. O. Box 9131, Berkeley, California 94709.

Times Literary Supplement. Admiral House, 66–68 East Smithfield, London E1 W 9BX England.

Tin House, poetry ed. Amy Bartlett. P. O. Box 10500, Portland, Oregon 97296.

TriQuarterly, ed. Susan Hahn. 2020 Ridge Ave., Evanston, Illinois 60208-4302.

Verse, eds. Brian Henry and Andrew Zawacki. English Dept., University of Georgia, Athens, Georgia 30602.

Volt, ed. Gillian Conoley. P. O. Box 657, Corte Madera, California 94976-0657.

ACKNOWLEDGMENTS

The series editor wishes to acknowledge his invaluable assistant, Mark Bibbins. Ideas or suggestions contributed by John Diamond-Nigh, Jennifer Factor, Stacey Harwood, Martha Kinney, Christine Korfhage, Rebecca Livingston, and Susan Wheeler were greatly appreciated. Warm thanks also go to Glen Hartley and Lynn Chu, of Writers' Representatives, and to Gillian Blake, Rachel Sussman, Giulia Melucci, Kim Hilario, Erich Hobbing, and Jay Schweitzer of Scribner.

Grateful acknowledgment is made of the editors of the publications from which the poems in this volume were chosen. Unless specifically stated otherwise, copyright to the poems is held by the individual poets.

Nin Andrews: "Notes for a Sermon on the Mount" appeared in *Another Chicago Magazine*. Reprinted by permission of the poet.

Rae Armantrout: "The Plan" appeared in *American Poetry Review*. Reprinted by permission of the poet.

John Ashbery: "Crossroads in the Past" from *Your Name Here*. Copyright © 2000 by John Ashbery. Reprinted by permission of the poet and Farrar, Straus and Giroux. First appeared in *New York Review of Books*.

Angela Ball: "Jazz" appeared in *The Nebraska Review*. Reprinted by permission of the poet.

Mary Jo Bang: "Crossed-Over, Fiend-Snitched, X-ed Out" appeared in *New American Writing*. Reprinted by permission of the poet.

Cal Bedient: "When the Gods Put on Meter" appeared in *Colorado Review*. Reprinted by permission of the poet.

Elizabeth Bishop: "Vague Poem" was first published in *The New Yorker*. Reprinted by permission of *The New Yorker* and of Farrar, Straus and Giroux.

Robert Bly: "The French Generals" from *The Night Abraham Called to the Stars*. Copyright © 2001 by Robert Bly. Reprinted by permission of the poet and of HarperCollins. The poem first appeared in *The Paris Review*. "Jesus at the Well" appeared in the *Times Literary Supplement* and is reprinted here by permission of the poet.

Lee Ann Brown: "Sonnet Around Stephanie" appeared in *Verse*. Reprinted by permission of the poet.

Michael Burkard: "Notes About My Face" from *Unsleeping*. Copyright © 2001 by Michael Burkard. Reprinted by permission of the poet and Sarabande Books. First appeared in *American Poetry Review*.

Trent Busch: "Heartland" appeared in *The Nation*. Reprinted by permission of the poet.

Amina Calil: "Blouse of Felt" appeared in *Faucheuse*. Reprinted by permission of the poet.

Bernard Welt: "I stopped writing poetry . . ." appeared in *The Antioch Review.* Reprinted by permission of the poet.

Dean Young: "Sources of the Delaware" appeared in *Volt.* Reprinted by permission of the poet.

Rachel Zucker: "In Your Version of Heaven I Am Younger" appeared in *American Poetry Review.* Reprinted by permission of the poet.